The *phat* Controller

(A Leadership Handbook)

Written by
Sean Langley *IRRV*

Order this book online at www.trafford.com/07-2849
or email orders@trafford.com

Most Trafford titles are also available at major online book retailers.

© Copyright 2008 Sean Langley.

All rights reserved. No part of this publication may be reproduced, stored in a retrieval system, or transmitted, in any form or by any means, electronic, mechanical, photocopying, recording, or otherwise, without the written prior permission of the author.

Cover Design: Jamie Sowler
Cover Photography: Graham Emery

Note for Librarians: A cataloguing record for this book is available from Library and Archives Canada at www.collectionscanada.ca/amicus/index-e.html

ISBN: 978-1-4251-6241-2

We at Trafford believe that it is the responsibility of us all, as both individuals and corporations, to make choices that are environmentally and socially sound. You, in turn, are supporting this responsible conduct each time you purchase a Trafford book, or make use of our publishing services. To find out how you are helping, please visit www.trafford.com/responsiblepublishing.html

Our mission is to efficiently provide the world's finest, most comprehensive book publishing service, enabling every author to experience success. To find out how to publish your book, your way, and have it available worldwide, visit us online at www.trafford.com/10510

www.trafford.com

North America & international
toll-free: 1 888 232 4444 (USA & Canada)
phone: 250 383 6864 ♦ fax: 250 383 6804
email: info@trafford.com

The United Kingdom & Europe
phone: +44 (0)1865 722 113 ♦ local rate: 0845 230 9601
facsimile: +44 (0)1865 722 868 ♦ email: info.uk@trafford.com

10 9 8 7 6 5 4 3 2

This book is dedicated to Pamela Campey
Much loved Aunt & Godmother,
who sadly passed-away whilst the book was in production.
The world is a poorer place without you.
God bless—you will be forever in my thoughts.

Co

Preface
- Invaluable 9

Introduction
- Terrorist Attacks 11
- Role Models 12
- Stepped Progression 13

Chapter 1 - Good Enough, is No Longer Good Enough !
- In the Beginning 15
- The Pace of Change 16
- The Second Derivative : Accelerate to Opportunity 18
- How Good Are Your Leaders ? 19
- The Cost of Failure 20

High *phat* Bites 21

Chapter 2 - Command & Control – the Last Bastion of Ineptitude ?
- Leadership Defined 23
- Integrity 24
- Command & Control 25
- Managing 'Upwards' 26
- Take Those Calls 27
- A Weak Form of Power 28
- Permission to Fly 28

High *phat* Bites 30

Chapter 3 - The Only Four Things That Really Matter
- Altruism 31
- Emotions 32
- Communication 34
- Words & Deeds 35

High *phat* Bites 37

Chapter 4 - The Golden Rule
- Actions Speak Louder Than Words 39
- Walk the Talk 40
- Low-Hanging Fruit 42
- Professionalism 43

High *phat* Bites 45

Chapter 5 – See the Bigger Picture
- Emotional Intelligence 47
- Stay on Message 48
- A Suitable Structure 50
- Involvement 51

High *phat* Bites 54

Chapter 6 – The Art of Listening
- Quality or Quality 55
- Delegation v Empowerment 57
- No Blame Culture 59
- A Recipe for Success 59
- Succession Planning 61

High *phat* Bites 62

Chapter 7 - Business Planning – the Missing Link
- A Proper Plan 63
- Business-Like 64
- A Blue-Print for Success 65
- Begin With the End in Mind 67
- Hard & Soft Skills 69

High *phat* Bites 70

Chapter 8 – Do Not Compromise on Quality
- Measure Outcomes, Not Activity 71
- Benchmarking 72
- Flexibility 73
- Stress Carriers 75

High *phat* Bites 77

Chapter 9 – Organise Yourself to Success
- Efficiency → Effectiveness → Excellence 79
- As Luck Would Have It 80
- Time Management 80
- Recruitment 82
- Retention 84

High *phat* Bites 86

Chapter 10 – Be True to Yourself
- Authenticity 87
- The Four Frameworks for Success 89
- The 'Cool' Leader (*phat* Controller) 92

High *phat* Bites 94

Acknowledgements & References 95

Index 97

Preface

INVALUABLE

I recall being asked by a couple of colleagues, back in the early 1990's, what my aims in life were. They commented that I did not appear to be very ambitious. Looks can be deceiving! I replied to the question posed by explaining that I really only had two aims. One was to be a good husband to my wife and the other was—should I ever have children—for them to consider me to be half as good a parent as mine had been to me, which would be a success.

Given that I failed with the first of those aims, I remain determined to succeed with the second. I am hopeful that my twin children, Natalie and Jack, will derive some pleasure and inspiration from the pages which follow in this book.

My parents, Barbara and Ken, have provided unwavering love and support throughout my life and, for that, I am eternally thankful. The loyalty that I share with my brothers, Paul and Gareth, is a source of tremendous re-assurance to me, and is something that I value enormously. It would be wrong of me to forget the role that both my previous wives, Liz and Tracey, have played in my life, and for that I am appreciative.

There are numerous friends and colleagues over the years that have helped in constructing my career and, ultimately formulating the thoughts and views I express in the following chapters. Too many to mention but, I hope they know who they are!

My professional body—The Institute of Revenues, Rating & Valuation (IRRV)—of which I have been a fully qualified Corporate member since 1985, has remained instrumental in my development.

In terms of this project, I would like to express my gratitude to my father, Ken, and to Professor Stanislaw Librowski for their contributions to, and critiquè of, the content of this book. They supplied totally invaluable advice in a pseudo-editorial role.

Finally, I should like to say a very special thank you to my partner, Monica; who has been a never-ending source of great love and encouragement to me. Indeed, it was Monica's suggestion that enthused me to write this book. I will be for evermore indebted to her for that, her motivation on this venture, and her companionship in life.

Introduction

TERRORIST ATTACKS

Frustrated by events going on in the world around me, in recent years I began to see a picture emerging of a lack of leadership, which was either contributing to some of the problems that existed or, was not helping in the aftermath of some of the incidents. Sometimes on an international scale, sometimes at national level, and sometimes only locally, as I observed issues I slowly became further perturbed. The more I thought about it, the more I wanted to write about a subject which, although complex at times, was not a science but, is very much an art.

It might help if, at this point, I give you an example of what I saw as effective, or opportune, leadership; together with an example of what I saw as ineffective, or inopportune, leadership.

The opportune example was the conduct of New York Mayor Rudolph Giuliani, in the aftermath of the September 11th terrorist attacks, on the twin World Trade Center towers, in 2001. He behaved with immense dignity and control, displaying an ability to sympathise sincerely with those who suffered most in the attacks whilst, at the same time, dealing appropriately with the inevitable attention from the World's media. He conveyed a strength and determination which his citizens, and probably most of the remainder of the US citizens, were able to draw upon for strength of their own.

The inopportune example was in the aftermath of the various terrorist attacks in the UK, which have taken place at various dates and venues since 2005. I believe that there should have been a very clear message from church leaders—both of the Muslim and the Christian faith—categorically condemning not only the actions themselves but, the fact that the actions were being claimed to be carried out in the name of God, or Allah. I have no wish to get involved in a religious debate but, even to me, it is quite evident that killing innocent people would not be an acceptable action in the scriptures of any religion. The whole world needed those religious leaders to come forward and make that absolutely clear. An opportunity to smooth the way forward has, therefore, been missed.

Although those examples are highly sensitive and extreme, the skills needed to be a good leader are eminently transferable, from a situation that involves millions of people allied to the intense media attention and scrutiny, right down to a team leader in an office. My intention is to draw upon my own experiences and learning, to develop a concept of how to be a leader in the modern world.

ROLE MODELS

This is a modern world in which, presently, I see a distinct lack of leadership. As I said right at the start, this ranges from on an international scale down to a local level, and across all sectors of society; public, private, business, commerce, education, sport, entertainment and, perhaps most significantly in, politics. There are no exemptions. The result of weak, or inadequate, leadership in society is a deterioration in standards of behaviour, manifested in a variety of guises.

By way of a modern example, like it or not owing to their public profile, professional sportsmen and women, particularly at the highest level, are role models. Unfortunately, picking on that with the highest profile, professional football fails miserably in its responsibility. The players themselves have a lot to answer for but, I have to say that the football authorities are equally culpable, by virtue of their failing to address the woeful standards of behaviour displayed by their 'product'.

On a more general level, and something that we can all identify with, you only have to look at some experiences of parenting to get an illustration of what I mean by inadequate leadership. These days some children get set such a poor example by their parents; others get set none at all. Whilst we—society generally—do not help ourselves; some respectable fathers, desperate to play a positive role in their children's lives, are prevented from even seeing their children. Simply crazy!

It has been suggested to me that the notion of 'Esprit de Corps' no longer exists, nor is relevant, in the modern world to which I have referred. So, why might this be? I strongly believe that the deficiencies in leadership through all facets of society, over several generations now, has led to an erosion of the values of human inter-dependence and support, which are embodied in this notion of 'Esprit de Corps'.

This has led to an 'every man for himself' attitude, permeating society now and spreading rapidly. I cannot help thinking back to the 1980's, when Margaret Thatcher and Ronald Reagan were at their most powerful; we were told that this somewhat ruthless, selfish approach, personified by those leaders, would come back to haunt us.

Maybe it has; ironic really, as I rated Thatcher highly as a leader when in office. But, I do feel that the scarcity of any meaningful leadership, whilst not directly contributing to, has certainly not helped challenge the growth in, for example, religious fundamentalism; the overwhelming stench of money, commercialism and materialism; the increase in aggressive attitudes (which is serving as an impostor for assertiveness); the way in which the influence of alcohol is somehow seen as an acceptable excuse for virtually anything; and the emergence of the 'brain-freezing' soap-opera/reality-TV/celebrity-driven banality of the entertainment world.

STEPPED PROGRESSION

However, all is not lost! I seriously believe that by applying the principles that I cover in the following pages, aspiring leaders will have the opportunity to re-assert the notion of 'Esprit de Corps', so far missed by the post second world war generations. I am setting out to explore some of, what I believe to be, the key issues to be faced in making the stepped progression from a follower to a 21st Century leader.

A follower is—reactive; observes and waits for things to happen.
A supervisor will—monitor; collect data and identify problems.
A manager can—plan; allocate resource and set targets.
A leader—motivates; inspires and creates vision.

The key issues to be faced apply whatever the field in which you work. Although my own experiences, upon which I draw heavily, have all been gained within an office environment within local government, I believe that a lot of what I discuss over the following pages and chapters transcends virtually all working environments. The skill-set required of a 'modern leader' would be transferable from one environment to another. I also make no apology for drawing analogies from the world of sport, to illustrate some of my points. So much of what happens in sports arenas and on sports fields—and, indeed, for that matter within dressing rooms—around the world that they are a microcosm for events that occur in the workplace. Consequently, I believe many lessons can be learnt by making (direct) comparisons.

In a series of chapters that range from Motivation through to Management of Performance, I will seek to examine these issues with a view to stimulating thought processes and, hopefully, inspire those leaders of tomorrow.

Chapter 1

GOOD ENOUGH, IS NO LONGER GOOD ENOUGH!

IN THE BEGINNING

As I turned to take the next flight of stairs, my gaze followed my boss as he led the path to the Director's Office. I listened intently as we climbed, trying to take everything in, when he half-turned and said to me, "I suppose the best advice I can give you is: Don't do as I do; do as I say!"

Many readers may recall similar stories from their own first day at work. I was eighteen years old and had just started working for the local council, as a trainee, eager to learn and was embarking on a career in revenue collection; which was later to transcend the Poll Tax era and subsequently Council Tax. So, although not to everyone's tastes, it was evidently not to be an uneventful career.

The question which I pose at this early stage is: how meaningful was that piece of advice offered by my very first boss? The answer is much more difficult to assess. What I consider to be such out-dated and old-fashioned thinking is surely dying out. Or is it?

Much has been, and much will continue to be written on the subject of Management and Management Thinking. The above is what I believe to be an example of an out-moded style of leadership, which should no longer hold up in the 21st Century organisation, where the customer is king and that *most* valuable of resources, the human kind, will exercise choice much more readily.

It is that exercising of choice more readily which should be exercising the thinking of managers. It should act as the catalyst for them to adopt a much more collaborative and inspirational approach or style. If, as a manager, you do not engage your staff, you *will* lose them; and all the money and resources that you have invested in training them, thus far, will be effectively money down the drain. So, I believe that, what in fact you should be looking for are people to "Do do as I do; do do as I say!" But, as a leader, you have to earn that opportunity; doing and saying the right things……all of the time.

My first boss was not at all bad. In fact, far from it. After all, still on my first day at work, he succeeded in sitting me down at a desk, opened up a grey book and, pointing at the page, he said, "Read that and learn it; it's probably the most important thing you need to know." I did as he said, and how right he was about that.

The grey book that he had given me was a book called 'Rating Law & Practice'. Not, I hasten to add, recommended for bed-time reading—unless you are keen to explore the aspects of 'Transient Occupation'—but, the book was widely recognised in our field as the essential guide and reference point for revenue collection practitioners. What my boss had pointed to was the explanation of a critical court case—esoterically known as the *John Laing* case!

THE PACE OF CHANGE

How things have changed in the intervening years since I started work in 1979—politically, the first of the (Margaret) Thatcher years! But the John Laing case, from 1949, is as the TV advert claims about Hovis—as good today as it's always been! The principles of the case, for the detail conscious amongst you, determined a convention for establishing liability to the old General Rates; and the findings still hold true for some aspects of both Business Rates and Council Tax today. It has long since proven to be essential knowledge—gained on my very first day at work; though little did I realise on that day just how essential it would become!

The pace of change, though, has accelerated and is now un-relenting. Sports enthusiasts amongst you will be familiar with Roger Black, a British Gold-medallist in the 4x400m relay team at the 1991 World Athletics Championships in Tokyo. Acceleration was something that he had in abundance.

Co-incidentally, Black's father was my own GP at the time I started work in Gosport in Hampshire, back in 1979. However, I digress, the former athlete earns his living these days as a motivational speaker, and in a speech to the Society of Chief Personnel Officers' annual conference, in Brighton in 2003, he told delegates that Local Government must be prepared to embrace change if it is going to move forward. Was he suggesting that the private sector already did so? I don't know but, I suspect that the answer may be that those commercial organisations which do not embrace change will simply go out of business. Like, it is claimed, there is no such thing as a poor bookmaker!

Roger Black: "the best will embrace change *generated by* their organisation; rather than change that *happens to* their organisation"

Many readers may be saying to themselves, "I do embrace change; in fact, I have no choice but to embrace it." True enough but, what Black was really alluding to, I believe, is that the best will embrace change *generated by* their organisation; rather than change that *happens to* their organisation. Much as that relay team, of which he was such a key member, did at those Tokyo games in 1991.

That team was at its peak during those championships but, still they had the immense courage to change (their running order) just before the final, in order to exceed expectations. Although the idea came from within the team itself, Black and his team-mates (Derek Redmond; John Regis and Kris Akabusi) embraced the logical thinking behind the proposed change and, as a result, they became world champions.

On paper, the United States relay team was superior. However, the move was designed to negate an advantage that the Americans had but, most importantly, to take advantage of the British team's major asset. The element of surprise it created to their competitors was crucial. I have heard both Black and Akabusi separately recount the story behind that triumphant day and, whilst you cannot fail to be moved by the emotion of the event, it underlines just what an extraordinary step it was to take at such a critical time.

THE SECOND DERIVATIVE: ACCELERATE TO OPPORTUNITY

Whilst on the subject of speed and acceleration, I came across an old article, in a Financial Times supplement, by Dr. Daniel Muzyka, who was Professor of Management at the University of British Columbia (Vancouver) at the time it was written. In it, he mentioned that it had been said "Mastering the first derivative is no longer sufficient; it is the second derivative that counts in…….competition". Translated, this roughly means that if you want to be successful, it is no longer your ability to demonstrate speed that is important; but your ability to accelerate quickly to capture an opportunity. I think the story above illustrates that point just about as perfectly as you could want it to.

As I have already touched upon, in the commercial sector under-performing managers are unlikely to experience a voyage of discovery but, more likely to steer their organisation onto the rocks. Although in the public sector, organisations are not necessarily in direct competition with each other, performance indicators and 'league tables' now mean that comparisons are made. 'Good enough', is no longer good enough!

So, whereas there are many, many managers in all fields that are very, very good managers; how many of those either can claim to be, or aspire to be, inspirational leaders? Who want to transform an organisation from one of average performance to one of peak performance? Who want to develop the leaders of tomorrow? Who want to be the 'Captains of Industry', sailing forth on a voyage of discovery? Who want to be at the forefront of our communities—locally, nationally and internationally? Who want to be 'the best'? Who want to master that second derivative?

The Institute of Human Development has stated that Transformational leaders need to learn how to:

- Build and purify a strong 'brand';
- Align their people to a single, compelling vision;
- Turn ordinary people into peak-performers;
- Develop a strong understanding of roles at all levels;
- Translate 'brand' values into core organisational behaviour.

None of these is easy to achieve but, by applying and adopting the principles discussed throughout this book, you will construct a convincing and persuasive case for success. Have you got the stomach for it?

HOW GOOD ARE YOUR LEADERS?

A lot of people know how to lead. Courses, lectures, seminars, books such as this, will all provide information on 'how' to do it. These days, you could probably even obtain the necessary information through an internet search engine. It can be learnt, that is true. If I believed that leaders were born and not made, there would be little point in writing this book. But, and this is a *big* but, how many people can *actually* do it? And, perhaps just as important, how many organisations measure prospective managers' capability to do it, as well as their officio managers' effectiveness at doing it? I think I can guess the answer to that!

My perception is that many organisations still generally remain guilty of the cliché, 'promoting people to their level of incompetence'. Are organisations looking closely enough at getting the most from their managers? They are, after all, a hugely significant resource. The impact of those managers MUST not be under-estimated.

An organisation can have all the tools in the box ready at their disposal, such as Investors in People accreditation, an established and effective Performance Management framework and, an appraisal system that links into both that and the Business Plan. However, if their managers are untrained in their use or, worse still, incapable of utilising them, then those tools can be rendered useless.

Managers can have a dramatic, as well as traumatic, effect on the performance of their team. We can all probably think of an instance of where we have either witnessed, or experienced, an example of 'bullying' by a more senior member of staff. Not necessarily physical but, possibly emotional. Was it not true to say that, although the victim may have felt compelled to work in order to satisfy their 'superior' officer—a travesty of language in such circumstances—the victim's performance was highly likely to be much better had they been working for a more effective 'leader', who was not a bully?

Managers can no longer just be symbolic. What I mean by that is, they cannot be nothing more than hyped-up team leaders or supervisors, and they cannot exist purely to sign off issues such as leave requests and check flexi-time sheets. In some industries, such as construction, they will have a critical health & safety role, anyway. However, whatever the field, they must get out and lead; provide the vision and guidance that staff crave. Humans *expect* to be managed but, they *desire* to be led.

Leadership is all about changing things…..for the better. If you don't change things, all you are doing is managing, or administering, a process. It is no longer acceptable to be just good at administration or organisation. Leadership skills need to be, not only evident but, to the fore. The practice of promoting people just because their time has come, and they are 'next in line', must stop……now!

THE COST OF FAILURE

Organisations must acquire a framework for identifying leadership aptitude, establish a programme for developing it and, essentially, design a methodology for measuring its success. For example, tools such as 360° appraisals may have had some bad press, and need nerve from all involved to derive maximum benefit from them but, it is obvious to me that they would play an integral part in assessing the effectiveness of a leader. How else would you know better whether a leader was communicating the vision, and providing the necessary guidance, than by asking those that they lead? Not forgetting that an appraisal is a mere tool in the box, not the panacea!

The issue here is that organisations need to invest time, effort and resource into identifying leadership talent—and I deliberately use the word 'leadership' rather than 'management'—and then developing it. The cost of not doing so is failure.

High *phat* Bites—Chapter 1

- If, as a manager, you do not engage your staff, you will lose them;
- The best will embrace change generated by their organisation; rather than change that happens to their organisation;
- 'Good enough', is no longer good enough;
- Humans expect to be managed but, they desire to be led;
- Organisations need to invest time, effort and resource into identifying leadership talent.

Chapter 2

COMMAND & CONTROL—THE LAST BASTION OF INEPTITUDE?

LEADERSHIP DEFINED

IF you aspire to be an inspirational, or transformational, leader you may be faced with making the step from being a follower to a leader, or maybe the smaller step from (good) manager to a leader. However, those could still be giant leaps; not quite of the same symbolic magnitude as Neil Armstrong's, when walking on the surface of the moon in 1969, but all the same for those of you involved, still giant.

It begs the question "what is a leader?" The word 'leader' first appeared in the English language in 1300, although there was no record of the use of 'leadership' until the beginning of the 19th Century. The Oxford English Dictionary defines it as "a person or thing that leads" or "a person followed by others". So, not a great deal of help in expanding our understanding of the word, I would suggest.

It is interesting to note that, although in English 'management' and 'leadership' are viewed as being different, the German word for management is 'führungskunst', which also translates as the art of leadership.

Is it, therefore, actually possible to define leadership? Is it really necessary to define leadership? It has been said that defining leadership is a bit like over-analysing a joke. If you picked it apart too much you would lose its essential quality. So, what is that essential quality?

I tend to agree that leadership, as a concept, is somewhat indefinable. To me 'Management' has an air of……'keeping things ticking-over'. 'Leadership', on the other hand, suggests……..something a little more dynamic!

For instance, it can be argued that Leadership will establish direction through having a vision, identify the required resources, align the key personnel and then motivate and inspire those personnel to get there. Management is what is required to plan and budget for that vision, organise the resources and monitor progress towards it—problem solving along the way, if necessary. Meanwhile, Leadership is already busy working on and towards the next vision! So, are you up to the challenge?

Psychologist Donald A. Laird had a simple test to measure leadership potential. He would ask five questions. Can you:

- take a reprimand without blowing up as a result?
- take a turndown without it allowing you to become discouraged?
- laugh along with others when the joke is actually on you?
- keep your spirits up when things go wrong (as, occasionally, they will)?
- keep your cool in an emergency?

If your answer is 'yes' to all five questions, I would venture to suggest that you are more than well on your way to being a leader. The late Dr. Laird advocated that the ability to keep cool in an emergency, to refuse to be stampeded, and to maintain poise in the midst of excitement, are the true marks of leadership.

INTEGRITY

You may become a leader when you stop blaming others for things going wrong. The buck stops with you, it is very important to not only understand that but, believe it! Some have demonstrated this aspect of leadership by absorbing any criticism that may come the way of their team, protecting them from it, but when praise is due, they always allow their staff to bask in it, rather than themselves.

To be a leader you must be visible and have vision; about which you are passionate and able to communicate eloquently. You must be professional in the way that you conduct yourself, especially with, and around, others. I have heard it said that when constancy; congruity; reliability and integrity are evident, you have the four ingredients of strong leadership. It is the latter ingredient which, above all, I believe is the vital quality that binds all of this together. Fail to have integrity and you fail as a leader!

What is interesting about that, as a concept, though is that I have an acquaintance—someone who is very well educated, well travelled and experienced in working in other countries and cultures—who is of the opinion that integrity is only really an issue in the western world. His, somewhat controversial, view is that the culture and infrastructure of other countries is less dependent on integrity and, possibly, more reliant on a type of 'who you know' environment. Perhaps in such an environment goals are achieved more through a combination of craft and stealth, as opposed to the development of a mutual trust, which can pave the way to success.

Not having worked in other cultures, I feel less qualified to express an opinion. However, I do find it very difficult to comprehend an environment in which there is a complete void of integrity; after all, we are all ultimately of the same race. May I suggest that integrity *is* necessary everywhere but, the key factor being that the level of integrity is measured by the follower? In other words, it will be measured relevant to, firstly, the culture or society in which the leader is operating and then, secondly, in the 'field' in which they are operating. Its defining features will be different in all circumstances.

Consequently, the nature of integrity is not necessarily transferable across cultures but, its existence is still necessary. Nevertheless, here in the UK, I am more intrigued by, what I perceive to be, an almost blind reliance on the hierarchical structure within organisations. I shall be looking at the relative importance, or not, of hierarchical structures later in Chapter Five but, it is the aspect of 'command & control', which stems from these hierarchical structures, that I would like to consider here.

COMMAND & CONTROL

'Freedom from Command & Control—a better way to make the work work', by John Seddon, is a fascinating book that explores the idea that command and control is no longer an effective methodology for modern day leaders, and well worth a read if you get the opportunity. If nothing else, I strongly urge you to read the Addendum. It is, in my opinion, a quite brilliant macro-analysis of all that is wrong with UK public service.

To para-phrase an entire book does it an enormous dis-service but, I would like to try and draw some very key conclusions from what I think are the issues that the book raises and examines. Essentially, what Seddon is saying is that the pre-occupation with targets, inspections and performance comparison 'league tables', that prevails in the UK—particularly the public sector—in the first decade of the 21st Century, adds no value to the work.

It can become a smokescreen behind which managers can hide, if they so choose. Instead of dealing with real issues and assisting the organisation to become more effective, they concentrate on hitting—sometimes meaningless—targets; in doing so, it has often proven to be human nature to cut corners.

In an environment where Health & Safety are paramount this could be, for example in the railway industry where cases such as the Cumbrian disaster in February 2007 have proven it to be, potentially catastrophic. These managers would be better advised to get closer to the work and find out what is really going on. In fact, what is being promoted here is what I believe to be a critical quality of leadership, 'getting your hands dirty'.

All staff need the re-assurance of knowing that their leader would be prepared, in an emergency or crisis, to do what they themselves have to do. Using an analogy; in the heat of a battle a leader may have to fight too! I have always been of the opinion that you should not ask your staff to do anything that you were not prepared to do yourself.

MANAGING 'UPWARDS'

Interestingly, as an aside, one of the benefits of *effective* leadership is that it provides the opportunity to lead those above you in a hierarchical structure. Just for the time being, I think we are relatively safe to assume that most organisations have some form of hierarchical structure. In order to take advantage of any opportunity to 'manage-upwards', you must display all those qualities identified by Donald A. Laird, referred to earlier in this chapter. A traditional command and control style does *not* afford you that luxury, as it relies heavily on an inflexible adherence to people's positions within the structure.

What do I mean by managing upwards? In the final Chapter of the book, I touch upon the understanding that, in certain situations, the hierarchical leader may not have the appropriate skill-set for every project that the organisation has to undertake. An example of what I am talking about here is that there will be times in your career when you wish to undertake a project, procure some attribute, or simply be a little creative, when you know that although it may not be in conflict with what your manager or your organisation's objectives are, it simply does not necessarily sit easily with them. But, you know it is key to your success. The issue may be as straightforward as budget provision and the ability to finance your 'project'.

Managing upwards does, however, require careful handling. It may necessitate a touch of subtlety, and not a little spirit, to be executed well. Your ability to convince your manager to go with your proposal, and allow you to lead the project, would be an illustration of your success at managing upwards.

Getting to know your manager, establishing an effective working relationship, communicating honestly and regularly, and you 'delivering the goods' will all help towards creating an environment where 'managing upwards' becomes possible. This is most likely to be in an environment where there is a strong element of mutual trust and/or respect.

TAKE THOSE CALLS

Talking of respect, over the years I have encountered a number of managers who seem to think that staff's respect is gained simply by virtue of position or status. Wrong! You have to earn it.

To illustrate this point; on many occasions I have seen and heard managers refusing to take calls from members of the public or customers who are demanding to speak to a manager. Quite alarming, really!

It brings to mind an anecdote I heard once about a council depot. As is fairly common, this depot closed to the public at 4:30pm on Fridays. It was now 4:20pm and the telephone rang.

"This is the Covdale Council Depot. I am sorry but there is no-one here to take your call, but if you'd like to leave a message please speak after the tone."

"Dave, is that you?"

"Tony?"

"Why are you pretending to be an answering machine, Dave?"

"I thought it might be a customer."

Now, I fully understand that, particularly in a customer driven environment, it is not likely that a manager would have the time to speak to everyone who called for them, and it is a balancing act, yes. But, they MUST speak to some callers, even if it is only a sample.

Why so? It will, in the first instance, provide an opportunity to hear at first hand from a customer's perspective what is 'going on' within your department, organisation, company or service. Secondly, it sends out a clear message to your staff that they *can* rely on their manager in a crisis; helping you to gain that much needed respect in the process.

As I said earlier in this chapter, in the heat of a battle a leader may have to fight too! Paradoxically, rather than taking advantage and putting more calls through, in my experience the vast majority of staff are more likely to 'protect' their manager in the future, assured in the knowledge that their manager will be there for them when really needed. This is common-sense, not rocket-science.

A WEAK FORM OF POWER

In Chapter One, I touched upon the realisation that, nowadays, the customer is king. But, do you hand on heart really adhere to that principle?

As Seddon says in his book, in order to be really effective in any business, and it applies equally to service organisations, we must see things from a customer perspective. The over-reliance on targets and inspections, that especially pervades the UK public sector currently, diverts attention from what really matters and stifles creativity in addressing that.

In order to be adjudged a success in the modern idiom, we must be flexible and responsive to customer needs and we must become leaders. Seddon suggests that the hierarchical command & control mentality that permeates UK local government, for instance, is counter-productive.

Unfortunately, UK local government also suffers at the hands of central government itself exerting this outdated command & control ethos. The proliferation of targets, performance indicators and inspections is ample evidence of that.

Command & control is, if challenged, a relatively weak form of power. Using position as a threat is unsustainable in the long term. As I also said in Chapter One, a bullying manager may get the work done but, I would be prepared to bet very heavily that it could be done better, quicker, cheaper or, more effectively were it being done not under duress. I go on to discuss the alternatives of the 'carrot or the stick' in Chapter Three. However, in my view, command & control has become the last bastion of ineptitude!

PERMISSION TO FLY

More effort must be put into doing the *right* things, rather than the *wrong* things righter. For example, using another local government issue to illustrate my point, if Housing Benefit notifications are so badly drafted that claimants fail to understand them, effort needs to be put into improving the notifications, not into putting more staff on the phone lines to deal with the complaints.

This might sound obvious to you as you read this but, it does not always happen. In one authority where I used to work, the local Benefits Agency, as it was called in the nineties, had more staff employed on the complaints line than assessing claims. Simply ludicrous! If it were not so serious a matter, it would be mildly amusing.

Seddon describes this as addressing 'failure' demand, rather than 'value' demand. Failure demand is essentially work created by your organisation's failure to do the right thing in the first place. For example, if you have made a promise to a customer, but failed to deliver, they are likely to create some 'failure demand' on you by contacting you to enquire 'why'. Failure demand is entirely wasteful and needs to be eradicated. By being responsive to customer needs you are much more likely to achieve this.

One major means of achieving this is to somehow give staff at all levels the licence to be creative and responsive to the needs of customers. As a leader you should be encouraging and permitting people to achieve: to perform to their highest potential, for their benefit and your organisation's. Let your team grow as individuals—give them 'permission to fly'—and you will undoubtedly see your team flourish as a unit. It has been said that it is not business that succeeds; it is the people in it!

Do you remember Robin Williams' performance in the role of Professor John Keating in my favourite film, Dead Poets Society? He jumped on the desk, during one lesson, to inspire his pupils to understand the benefit of looking at things from a different angle. I return to this point later, in Chapter Six.

If you always do what you have always done—you will always get what you have always got! That may not necessarily always be a bad thing but, by doing that, will you be inspirational or, indeed, transformational?

High *phat* Bites—Chapter 2

- Leadership will establish direction through having a vision;
- Fail to have integrity and you fail as a leader;
- Command and control is no longer an effective methodology for modern day leaders;
- More effort must be put into doing the right things, rather than the wrong things righter;
- Failure demand is entirely wasteful and needs to be eradicated.

Chapter 3

THE ONLY FOUR THINGS THAT REALLY MATTER

ALTRUISM

THERE is no such thing as a purely altruistic act; or so it is claimed. If I added the word "Discuss" after that initial sentence, it could be mistaken for an interesting question from a Psychology examination paper. It has also been suggested that, at work, people only do things for one of two reasons. Either to gain personal reward or, to avoid personal punishment. In other words, the carrot or the stick.

On the basis that an effective leader is much less likely to generate a feeling of fear in his team, it follows therefore, that the first alternative—the carrot—is much more likely to achieve the desired results. A truly effective leader could even generate results that are beyond, or better, than expectations.

As an aside, but related to just that point, I am writing this book in 2007, when Roy Keane is relatively new to his post as Manager at Sunderland Football Club. He played under two of the most successful and influential club managers in the history of English football, Sir Alex Ferguson and the late Brian Clough. Although Keane spent more time in his career playing under Ferguson, I would venture to suggest that it is Clough from whom he will draw the greatest benefit and thus influence his own style. The reason I say this is that Clough had to achieve success in arguably more difficult circumstances—not having the financial clout that Ferguson has had at Manchester United. In other words, Clough's hand at Nottingham Forest and Derby County was much more similar to the hand that Keane has been dealt at Sunderland. Clough clearly delivered results that were better than expected; it could be argued that Ferguson has only delivered what was expected!

However, for the purposes of clarifying the earlier point, personal reward does not include financial reward. So, what might it include? Personal professional development would be high on the list. It is true to say that everyone should take responsibility for their own development but, an effective leader will take the initiative to assist and collaborate with their staff in plotting their own career development. Having a professional development plan in place enables staff to understand the speed at which they may progress within that organisation and, therefore, helps manage expectations. Very often new and additional responsibilities that are linked to such a plan will be just as important to people as would any new job title or salary increase.

In the modern workplace, the other significant 'carrot' which has begun to be harvested is flexible working arrangements. With the heavy focus on getting the work/life balance right, working patterns are of utmost importance. Whether that be part-time hours; flexi-time; job-sharing; shift-working or, even working from home; leaders who can demonstrate a willingness to be flexible will reap rich reward in retaining and inspiring quality staff. I return to this point later in Chapter Eight.

EMOTIONS

In an article called 'One more time—How do you motivate employees?', published in the late 1960's in the Harvard Business Review, the late Frederick Herzberg argued that you *cannot* motivate someone. "You can provide conditions in which employees are more likely to be motivated or demotivated but, it is a conceit to believe that managers can motivate people. It is stretching credulity to believe that a target, set in a hierarchical system, imposed by those above on those below, is something that people would find motivational." Does that resonate with you as much as it does with me? An interesting angle, and one with which I do not disagree.

But, if what Herzberg said is the case, why would any of us bother aspiring to be transformational leaders? What is in it for leaders, why would they put the effort in if people cannot be motivated? Does the carrot or the stick not apply just as much to managers? To a certain extent, yes it does. However, in my experience, the answer is that what we should be seeking to do is *inspire* people. Succeed in doing that and they will *motivate* themselves. Semantics? Maybe!

Martin Luther King Jr.: "I Have a Dream"

What I am saying is that an effective leader will, by their words and their deeds, trigger a motivated response borne out of inspiration to achieve. Whatever that achievement is, that is the personal reward talked about earlier, and results will have been attained not through any form of threat or fear.

Research has shown that the way to inspire people is through their emotions! This is the trick that all great leaders through time have mastered. Humans are driven by their emotions—ego, self-esteem, pride, dignity to name but a few. Therefore, by appealing to these senses, a leader is much more likely to succeed. However, do beware! It is possible to appeal to people's emotions in a negative way—by exercising the 'threat' that I have previously referred to in the traditional command & control environment. Falling into this trap will result in you failing to inspire your team.

To achieve success, what you must do is appeal to the emotions in a positive way. Trade Union leaders, such as Arthur Scargill, have succeeded in doing this consistently over the years, by playing what amounts to the 'solidarity brothers' card. Other great public addresses that inspired millions of people, such as Martin Luther King Jr.'s "I have a dream!", and Sir Winston Churchill's "We shall never surrender!", used the same type of rallying call but, in much different circumstances. Almost emotional blackmail one might say.

COMMUNICATION

I once attended a lecture by Denis Beard, Director of Management at the University of Reading, at the time. He suggested that what makes people tick is to feel important, to be considered important and, not to lose face.

In the work-place, I believe the secret to accomplishing this is through involvement and communication. We will have a look at involvement later in the book but, I wanted to spend a little time considering the thorny issue of communication. Thorny, because every organisation I have ever been involved with has, at some stage, been criticised by those within it for poor communication. I am including both work related and social organisations in that sweeping statement. Without fail, they have all got it wrong at some point. Are the organisations with which you are involved any different?

It is true to say that it is very difficult to succeed in effective communication. Too little and you are accused of hiding something or, having a hidden agenda; too much and you are accused of wasting time, effort and resources. But, in very simple terms, it is better to over-communicate than under-communicate. Once people have access to information, it is their decision whether they choose to take note and use it. The crucial thing is that you have empowered them to make that choice.

Yet, I am not at all surprised that many organisations fail in effective communication. I am constantly exasperated, for example, at the inability of car drivers to indicate appropriately on our roads. It is not that they get it wrong; they just do not do it at all. It is, quite literally, criminal that so many drivers are ignorant, inconsiderate and selfish, when in control of a potential killing-machine; because, let us be honest, that is what a car is. It is hardly an onerous task to turn an indicator on in a modern car, is it? Just flick that switch. And, in the vast majority of situations, the car will even switch it off for you afterwards! Oh, the effort! But, time after time, it fails to happen. People simply cannot be bothered to do it, failing to understand that such a simple action can make things so much easier (and safer!) for other road users.

I digress but, an important issue all the same. The point that I am making is that if people are so lazy as to not be bothered to communicate in, what can amount to be, such critical (life or death even) circumstances, what chance have we got that it will happen in the work-place? For the effective leader though, the law is communicate, communicate, communicate......even if it is bad news. Much as with a car, keep doing it and eventually, it will become habit. A good habit to have, too.

Employees will respect honesty and they cannot abide being kept in the dark. Most importantly, ensure that you regularly undertake face-to-face communication, not via e-mail—especially if it is bad news. One of the biggest enemies of staff morale is ambiguity. By communicating face-to-face you are much more likely to transmit a clear message, for two main reasons.

The first is body language. It is an established fact that an incredibly high proportion of effective communication, something approaching eighty percent, is achieved through body language. A genuine or sincere smile is very difficult to convey in an e-mail, for instance. The written word is fraught with potential for misunderstanding. So, do not underestimate the significance of this and take every possible opportunity to meet with your team face-to-face.

The second is the opportunity for questions. By meeting face-to-face, should there be any misunderstandings, you are giving people the chance to ask questions and seek clarification, minimising the risk of any ambiguity arising.

Oh, and one other thing. Staff prefer to hear news from their *own* line manager, not a Director that they perhaps only see on a walk-about at Christmas. Hearing news directly from their own line manager makes it seem much more real and personal. So, a good exercise in direct cascading of information through an organisation, quickly and accurately, will go a long way to limiting any criticism.

WORDS & DEEDS

I once, at a staff meeting in the midst of crucial preparations in a major tendering exercise, explained to the team why I had to make a particular decision, endeavouring to reassure them by promising that I would keep them informed as much as I possibly could. I sincerely believed that they deserved nothing less. After my explanation, I asked them if there were any questions. After a brief pause, one colleague said that if I were to keep my promise, as a group they could expect no more of me. Nothing more was said, nor need it have been.

This was an example of effective communication. When I stop and analyse it, what I did was I made people feel important by involving and informing—and I appealed to their emotions, by explaining that we were all in it (tendering for our existence) together. I had explained that the decision to which I was referring was being taken with the group's best interests at heart.

Earlier, I referred to a leader triggering a motivated response through their words and deeds. I have heard it said that there are only four things that matter in leadership:

What you say………and how you say it;

What you do……….and how you do it.

Perhaps a little over-simplification but, all the same, I think that is a perfect summary of the significance of words and deeds and, so simple, that it needs no explanation. A transformational, or inspirational, leader will never forget that adage and, if their words and deeds are infused with sincerity and integrity, they *will* inspire.

High *phat* Bites—Chapter 3

- Having a professional development plan in place enables staff to understand the speed at which they may progress within that organisation;
- An effective leader will, by their words and their deeds, trigger a motivated response borne out of inspiration to achieve;
- What makes people tick is to feel important, to be considered important and, not to lose face;
- It is better to over-communicate than under-communicate;
- One of the biggest enemies of staff morale is ambiguity.

Chapter 4

∽

THE GOLDEN RULE

ACTIONS SPEAK LOUDER THAN WORDS

In the previous chapters, I have discussed the idea that the customer is king and, that good enough is no longer good enough. Emphasised that the call is for transformational leaders; command & control no longer works and you should aim to be inspirational. Towards the end of Chapter Three, I stated that there are only four things that really matter:

What you say.........and how you say it;
What you do..........and how you do it.

I now want to explore the significance of those four things and how they need to remain a constant thread through all that you do. This develops into the notion of leading by example. In fact, it brings me back full circle to where I began in Chapter One, and that story of my first day in the office.

If you remember, I was told, "Don't do as I do, do as I say!" Yet, on the other hand, is it not the case generally that 'actions speak louder than words'? If you need any convincing of that, then read the following tale, which I came across in a neat little publication by the Economics Press (UK) Ltd.

A little girl, whose parents had died, lived with her grandmother and slept in an upstairs bedroom.

One night there was a fire in the house and the grandmother perished while trying to rescue the child. The fire spread quickly, and the first floor of the house was soon engulfed in flames.

Neighbours called the fire service, and then stood helplessly by, unable to enter the house because the flames blocked all the entrances. The little girl appeared at an upstairs window, crying for help, just as word spread among the crowd that the firefighters would be delayed a few minutes, because they were all at another fire.

Suddenly, a man appeared with a ladder, put it up against the side of the house, and disappeared inside. When he reappeared he had the little girl in his arms, he delivered the child to the waiting arms below, then disappeared into the night.

An investigation revealed that the child had no living relatives, and weeks later a meeting was held in the town hall to determine who would take the child into their home and bring her up.

A teacher said she would like to raise the child. She pointed out that she could ensure her a good education. A farmer offered her an upbringing on his farm. He pointed out that living on a farm was healthy and satisfying. Others spoke, giving their reasons why it was to the child's advantage to live with them.

Finally, the town's richest resident arose and said, "I can give this child all the advantages that you have mentioned here, plus money and everything that money can buy."

Throughout all this, the child remained silent, her eyes on the floor.

"Does anyone else want to speak?" asked the meeting chairman. A man came forward from the back of the hall. His gait was slow and he seemed in pain. When he got to the front of the room, he stood directly before the little girl and held out his arms. The crowd gasped. His hands and arms were terribly scarred.

The child cried out, "This is the man who rescued me!" With a leap, she threw her arms around the man's neck, holding on for dear life, just as she had that fateful night. She buried her face on his shoulder and sobbed for a few moments. Then she looked up and smiled at him.

"This meeting is adjourned," said the chairman.

Scarcely believable but, very moving all the same. Sad to think that nothing so human would be permitted to happen in today's politically correct, disinfected world. However, the point of the tale is there for all to see. So, which of the four things that really matter, matters most?

WALK THE TALK

Lest we should forget the significance of Harry Potter in popular culture, did not Professor Dumbledore, in the film 'The Chamber of Secrets,' state to the young wizard that "it is not our skills that make us what we are; it is our choices"? In other words, what we choose to do speaks volumes to others about 'what we stand for'!

I think that that is fine and, as a personal or individual maxim, is very credible. However, as a leader you become responsible for the deeds of others; so you need to, not only, demonstrate your commitment by actions, you must be able to communicate your vision effectively. Otherwise, your team's deeds may be at best unco-ordinated; at worst, counterproductive or even destructive. Do not take that risk!

By applying the 'four things that really matter' you will understand and appreciate that *both* words *and* deeds are crucial as a leader. And, to use a cliché, you must walk the talk!

I never cease to be amazed at how many managers seem to propagate their own negative experiences. What I mean by this is that it seems to be that they once felt mistreated in the workplace, as they fought their way up the hierarchical structure, so they want to exercise their power in some sort of apparent exorcism of the past, by mistreating their own subordinates. I do not think anyone would argue that it is justifiable to abuse your child, just because you were abused as a child yourself. So, why is it acceptable in the work-place to perpetuate those negative conditions?

In an episode of ITV's hugely successful television series, Coronation Street, which was broadcast on British television on 5th December 2005, the character Keith Appleyard talked about the most important thing in life being self-respect. He explained that to *not* have to do things that you do not agree with, or feel uncomfortable with, is important. How true! Occasionally, in the workplace, this can be an issue (those working in Local Government finance in the UK in the early nineties need little to remind them of the Poll Tax!). Therefore, an effective leader will, by their words and deeds, make it *less* likely that staff will feel that they have to do something that they feel uncomfortable with.

In leadership, the Golden Rule should be applied: "Do unto others as you would have done unto yourself". It is essential that leaders are able to recognise how critical their role is in creating a positive environment, within which the individual parts (staff) can flourish for the benefit of the whole (organisation). As a leader you may need to change to achieve it and have the courage to identify if you are yourself a stress-carrier.

I guess that much of what I am saying could even be traced back to Dale Carnegie's 1936 book, "How to Win Friends and Influence People". Regrettably, this might appear to be in direct contrast to many modern day theories that the reader may have experienced, in which the importance of assertiveness is propagated. I do not believe that 'The Golden

Rule' is incompatible with assertiveness at all. On the contrary; but this should not, however, be confused with aggression. Aggressive traits as a leader will become counter-productive, whereupon you WILL be a stress-carrier. In my view the title of Carnegie's book hits the nail on the head. In a non-aggressive way!

LOW-HANGING FRUIT

Coming more up-to-date, Stephen Covey in his book "The Seven Habits of Highly Effective People" talks about this and describes it as "a principle-centred, character-based, *inside-out* approach to personal and interpersonal effectiveness".

He explains that you can apply either the character-ethic or, the personality ethic. The character-ethic is the more deep-rooted and fundamental approach, applying integrity, humility, fidelity, temperance, courage, justice, patience, industry, simplicity, modesty and the golden rule. The personality ethic is a more superficial quick-fix approach, image consciousness with a liberal application of human or public relations techniques, plus positive mental attitude.

In very modern-parlance, the personality ethic is known as picking at the low-hanging fruit; where the aim is to achieve the maximum gain, for the minimum effort. However, beware. Easy targets are not always what they seem. Fruit-farmers will tell you that only inexperienced pickers go for the fruit lower down, where it is less likely to see the sun and be less ripe. In management, or leadership terms, it may make better sense to tackle the bigger issues first—co-incidentally, an issue which Covey also deals with.

You may be able to massage the figures (whatever they may be in your chosen field) by which your performance is measured, through applying the personality ethic in the short-term. However, for long-term sustained success you have to apply the character ethic, which can be supplemented with some aspects of the personality ethic, if you so wish.

Further, Covey urged, "Change—real change—comes from the inside out. It doesn't come from hacking at the leaves of attitude and behaviour with quick-fix personality ethic techniques. It comes from striking at the root—the fabric of our thought, the fundamental, essential paradigms, which give definition to our character and create the lens through which we see the world".

In his autobiography, Anwar Sadat, the former Egyptian leader, concurred with this view, stating "he who cannot change the very fabric of his thought will never be able to change reality and will never, therefore, make any progress".

PROFESSIONALISM

Covey's book, and the course that accompanies it, has had the most profound effect on my life of any course or book that I have ever experienced. If you get the opportunity, I advocate that you experience them for yourself. In fact, no! I implore you to take time to do so!

It is Covey's character-ethic ideology that is at the core of what I am trying to say throughout this, my own book. Particularly here, where I am seeking to explain the sheer enormity of the importance of infusing your words and deeds with integrity, sincerity and a hefty dose of professionalism.

In order to demonstrate what I am talking about when I say 'professionalism', may I use a couple of examples? These will hopefully illustrate how a thoroughness for doing the right thing, can transmit a very strong message to those both inside and outside of your organisation.

The first example is dealing with an issue and communicating that. Staff get exasperated and deflated by managers who seek to address a problem (e.g. perpetual lateness) by instructing, or re-instructing, *all* staff, rather than just the perpetrator. Deal with the issue directly and communicate accordingly, if you must. For example, you could issue an e-mail, in the aftermath of an 'incident', saying "I have recently dealt with a member of staff for *(insert problem)*; consequently I am *(insert instruction)*". In this way, the individual involved has their confidentiality maintained and, staff generally at least know that the issue has been dealt with directly, and they have not all been 'tarred with the same brush'. The underlying message also gets re-affirmed in a sort of subliminal way.

The second example is appraisals, or performance reviews. Once you set a date and time for a staff members review, never *ever* cancel it except in an emergency. For 'emergency', read 'in event of death'! By setting a date and time and then sticking to it, you send a very strong message to your staff that they *are* your most important asset. Quite honestly, if you are asked by your manager, or the Chief Executive, or the Director to do something that would require you to change an appraisal appointment, you must be strong and explain to them why you cannot do that. If they do not understand why, then they do not deserve to have an inspired body of staff working for them!

The third example is complaints. In some working environments, complaints are plentiful. Some justified, many not. However, how many of you have ever picked up the complaints file and, some time after the complainant has received their reply, have you contacted them and asked were they satisfied at the time and, are they satisfied now? Such actions would convey a very strong message to them (the customers) that you mean it, when you say they are important. Make sure your staff know that you do it, too. The customer is king! Make them believe it—make your staff believe it!

A key point I should like to emphasise here is, achieving all of that to which I have referred in this chapter cannot be done overnight. It may take years of hard work and effort to instil confidence in your team and convince them of the depth of your conviction. But, for lasting success and to be a transformational, inspiring leader, persevere you must.

Mahatma Ghandi was once quoted as saying: "It's the action, not the fruit of the action that's important. You have to do the right thing. It may not be in your power, may not be in your time, that there'll be any fruit. But that doesn't mean that you stop doing the right thing. You may never know what results from your action. But if you do nothing, there will be no result."

High *phat* Bites—Chapter 4

- What we choose to do speaks volumes to others about what we stand for;
- Aggressive traits as a leader will become counter-productive;
- For long-term sustained success you have to apply the 'character ethic';
- A thoroughness for doing the right thing, can transmit a very strong message to those both inside and outside of your organisation;
- It may take years of hard work and effort to instil confidence in your team and convince them of the depth of your conviction.

Chapter 5

SEE THE BIGGER PICTURE

EMOTIONAL INTELLIGENCE

READERS who have delved into James Redfield's interesting and thought-provoking book, 'The Celestine Prophecy', will doubtless have little trouble recalling the rather unique story. It revolves around the pursuit of the Ninth Insight into the development and evolution of spiritual thinking in human-kind.

I am not going to go all spiritual on you right now but, in the chapter from the book about the Eighth Insight, Redfield describes a way of consciously relating to our fellow man, "in which everyone attempts to bring out the best in others, rather than to have power over them". He goes on to suggest that this "is a posture the entire human race will eventually adopt". At this juncture, rather excitedly, one of his book's characters says, "Think of how everyone's energy level and pace of evolution will increase at that point!" Indeed, quite a thought.

As likeable and endearing a picture as that image conjures, it sounds more like an advert for Utopia, probably with John Lennon's brilliant song, 'Imagine', being played as the back-drop! However, it does raise a crucial issue for leaders, which is the core of this chapter—that of bringing out the best in others, rather than exerting power.

Leaders cannot achieve things by themselves. As we have previously discussed, great leaders will have the ability to inspire people to work to the common goal. Writer Daniel Goleman believed that leaders require what he described as 'emotional intelligence'. This is a relatively new concept, with definitions and research regarding its validity continuing to evolve.

Nevertheless, the on-line encyclopedia, Wikipedia, describes Emotional Intelligence as 'an <u>ability</u>, capacity, or <u>skill</u> to perceive, assess, and manage the emotions of one's self, of others, and of groups'. Goleman himself expressed it as the ability to be both self-aware and self-regulating, whilst at the same time being both compassionate and empathetic.

Either way, simplifying it, I think that it is a scientific way of explaining that someone has a skill for understanding themselves and others, and the inter-relationships that develop. Being so skilled would enable you to hear what you need to know and inspire others in what they need to do. I refer back to this in Chapter Ten.

As well as having the emotional intelligence to accomplish the common goal, a leader also needs a framework for facilitating it—through a formal structure and team-work. This is particularly so in larger organisations, otherwise chaos would reign.

STAY ON MESSAGE

I have seen a formal organisation described as 'a pattern of senior-subordinate relationships, with authority and command lines converging on the chief executive. It is a sequence of formal relationships grouped within a hierarchical structure, the purpose of which is to effectively achieve specified results, through a series of inter-related activities'. Accurate; but hardly rolls off the tongue, does it?

In the early 20th Century, Max Weber wrote much about bureaucracy and explained that corporate relationships were based on authority and subordination. At the time, only a lucky few members of the general public had access to higher education, which in turn led them to the higher positions in business, industry and commerce; such as it was back then. Companies needed complex structures because most people were uneducated and could, therefore, only handle the more simple jobs. Of course, this no longer holds true but, the hierarchical structures remain and, for the most part, seem to work.

However, in order to succeed, everyone in the chain has to play their part. A chain is only as strong as its weakest link, they say; but, I have been astonished on several occasions to discover, within some organisations, that individuals within the chain remain ignorant of that simple fact. In Chapter Four, I talked about people needing to feel important and to be considered important. You would go a long way to achieving this, if you took the first opportunity to make sure that everyone was aware that they *are* important and, if they foul-up, it affects everyone else. This should not be done, though, with the intention of putting pressure on people. Hold true to the carrot, not the stick!

It is also worth remembering that a message of such great magnitude may have to be repeated several times to get the message across and to instil in people the belief that you do actually mean what you are saying. Nevertheless, some people will still mis-understand, some will still be mis-believing and some will be just plain missing! Stay on message, re-inforce it and live it.

What I mean by that is demonstrate, in everything that you do and say, that people are important— walk the talk. Take an interest in people and their lives and, where appropriate, make sure they know that you appreciate the good work they are doing. You will not achieve any of this by sitting in your office, just sending out e-mails, and being critical without balancing it with thanks. Get out there and lead!

To me, this is allied to the significance of staff not only seeing but, understanding, the bigger picture. It is obvious, I would have thought, that staff are more likely to be effective in undertaking their duties when they appreciate the reasons why they are doing it. This applies to the most basic of procedures, as much as it does to any strategy.

If it is explained why there is a very good reason envelopes need to be put into the post-tray address-side down, for example; that requirement is much more likely to be complied with than when staff enquire "why?", and are simply told "because that's how it's always been done". Understanding focuses the mind and frees up the imagination.

At a much higher level, I find it deeply disturbing when, for instance, assessment staff in a Council's Benefits assessment office are unable to recognise that they are as much responsible for fraud detection as are their colleagues in the anti-fraud team. Similarly, where the billing staff in the Council Tax team are unable to identify that they are accountable for the collection rate, just as much as their recovery colleagues.

Seeing the bigger picture links right back in to having a vision and being able to communicate it. Crack that little nut and you will be able to create an environment where staff know what the bigger picture is— the corporate vision. It will become a covert part of their everyday life, underpinning everything they do, without them even thinking about it, necessarily.

A SUITABLE STRUCTURE

Now, after my veiled attack on 'command & control' earlier in the book, you could have been forgiven for thinking that I have little regard for hierarchical structures in any shape or form. Not so!

I do recognise that there is a need for some form of command chain; otherwise the work-place would degenerate into anarchy. Given, too, that my father was in the Royal Navy, I would be somewhat naive to fail to understand that command & control must exist in both the armed forces and the emergency services through necessity; potentially a matter of life or death.

But why, in a business environment, do we need formal structures? The simple answer is that there is no known (better) alternative.

A number of you reading this will have had the opportunity to attend those management courses where you role-play being stranded on a desert island, and you have to work out how to survive. The moral behind that role-play is, of course, that there will more than likely be an evolvement of a natural leader and structure; with team work emerging that capitalises on individual strengths, to create a synergistic and triumphant environment.

That is the theory; although William Golding's story 'Lord of the Flies' may dispute that. In reality, though, you cannot rely on team-work being created or emerging, at will, in a crisis. I guess an element of a 'siege mentality' may develop and people may pull together but, do not count on it. It would be much better were it something that you were continuously building and working towards on a daily basis.

A formal organisation does not have to exert power but, it does enable the effective implementation of appropriate decisions, and allows the strength(s) of individuals to be nurtured, channelled and utilised.

What I do believe though, is that there needs to be more fluidity in hierarchical structures, in order to be more receptive to business need. The public sector, for instance, is generally too hung-up on structure and in my own field, Local Government, they need to respond more rapidly to the world in which they now operate. The difficulty that readers may face is that, in any organisation, a change of this nature really needs to come, and be led, from the very top; with the opportunity to become either more business-like or more competitive being limited, unless the organisation as a whole embraces this mind-set.

INVOLVEMENT

I experienced this a few years ago when, working for a local authority, I succeeded with an in-house bid in a tendering exercise, for the very work that my team of about fifty staff were already undertaking. Now, that was pressure! In an environment where I would have said that it was unusual, to say the least, to be this way, I had adopted what I thought was a more business-like approach. To begin with, I was actively encouraged to do so by my seniors, and I honestly believed that it was crucial for our very survival. However, in time, it became apparent that this was only acceptable 'after a fashion'.

That authority's Direct Services Manager, responsible for maintenance of parks and open spaces, had operated in a tendering environment for a number of years and his experience was a resource that I was keen to tap into. During a conversation with him one day, he explained that his staff would work forty hours per week in the summer, when they were busier and the light provided more opportunity to work, and they worked thirty-four hours per week during the winter; whilst getting paid for thirty-seven hours per week all year round.

There were some minor problems to overcome, such as working out the effect of the Christmas close-down period on contractual hours and, staff joining and leaving during the course of the year but, the approach was that this would all just come out in the wash—you win some, you lose some. These minor details were not show-stoppers and the overall result was far more important than getting hung-up on some slight imperfection in the model; which, unfortunately, was often the way in Local Government, as one might imagine. Back to John Lennon again!

John Lennon: "Imagination!"

The system which he described struck a chord with me for, in the work that I was responsible for—revenue collection and benefit assessment, it was far busier from February through to July, encompassing the annual billing exercise for Council Tax and Business Rates, end-of-financial-year accounts, beginning of the new rent year et al. Then, from August round to January it was less busy. I emphasise that I did not say 'not busy', I said 'less busy'! Adopting a similar system to our Direct Services Manager would have enabled me to overcome a major peak of work whilst managing to minimise overtime costs; such as during financial year-end/annual billing, for example.

Do you remember me saying in Chapter Three that I tried to involve my staff in decision-making? This was a good example. When I addressed them on the matter they agreed that it would be a sensible approach. How rewarding and refreshing it was for me to see that they, too, were not hung-up on the detail, given that they might miss out on some overtime, but they could see that it was better for the whole section looking at the bigger picture. So, armed with this backing, I took it to the authority. Astonishingly to me I was turned-down because, it was explained to me, staff elsewhere in the organisation might want to do similar!

My response to that was that if it made operational sense then why would you not want them to do it? But, this was Local Government and I was not to succeed on this issue. 'Frustrated' was an understatement! Despite having nurtured the team's support through involvement in the decision-making process, the plan was thwarted through, what I perceived to be, archaic mind-sets, and a failure by senior management themselves to see the bigger picture.

Although the approach I was proposing would have been a pretty radical one for 'white-collar' staff; by being turned down I had not been empowered by the formal organisation to implement an appropriate 'decision'. It had, unfortunately, exerted its power and the result was, in my opinion, a missed opportunity to help bring out the best in my team.

High *phat* Bites—Chapter 5

- Great leaders will have the ability to inspire people to work to the common goal;
- Demonstrate, in everything that you do and say, that people are important;
- Understanding focuses the mind and frees up the imagination;
- You cannot rely on team-work being created or emerging, at will, in a crisis;
- The overall result is far more important than getting hung-up on some slight imperfection in a model.

Chapter 6

∞

THE ART OF LISTENING

QUALITY OR QUALITY?

THE 'quality' revolution that most businesses have had to embrace since the 1990's may yet be just one more example of what staff generally term 'the current management fad'.

Fad it certainly is not, because a lot of what occurs can be imposed from above, e.g. central government. On top of which, have I missed something along the way; have we not always sought quality?

I remember being taught a long time ago, as an analogy for business, about the difference between a Rolls Royce Silver Shadow service and a Ford Cortina (remember them?) service. Both are quality, otherwise they would not have enjoyed longevity, but on very different levels. In business terms, the idea was that you need to determine whether you were going to provide a Rolls Royce Silver Shadow level service or, a Ford Cortina level. You 'cut your cloth' accordingly. It certainly is an analogy that focuses the mind on, what is, a very important point. The significant difference nowadays, though, is that there has definitely been a success in focusing the service on the customer, and what the customer perceives to be quality. That perception may be totally different to that of the service provider.

So, do not forget—the customer is king!

The quality culture spawned in the 1990's required continuous improvements through change and better value for money, achieved with less staff and flatter hierarchical structures. This has been manifested in trends such as the International Organisation of Standardisation (ISO); Total Quality Management (TQM), Compulsory Competitive Tendering (CCT), Best Value, Comprehensive Performance Assessment (CPA) and now, in local government they are faced with the Gershon and the Varney agendas, amongst others.

Perhaps the most talked about model at the time of writing is the Balanced Scorecard (BSC) approach, which had its origins as far back as 1990. Of course, we should not forget the European Foundation for Quality Management's (EFQM) continued push, for businesses throughout Europe to adopt the Business Excellence Model (BEM). A number of organisations are utilising facets of both the BSC and BEM models, as they are capable of being transposed.

I do not wish to appear dismissive of such models but, I am afraid that despite strenuous assertions otherwise, most of these types of schemes do end up becoming somewhat transient. They are all really just commonsense, re-mixed by the latest DJ (Development-model Junkie). However, it is also true to say that they have all got something meritorious about them to a greater or lesser degree. So, perhaps I may be permitted to dwell on the BEM for just a moment.

BEM Model

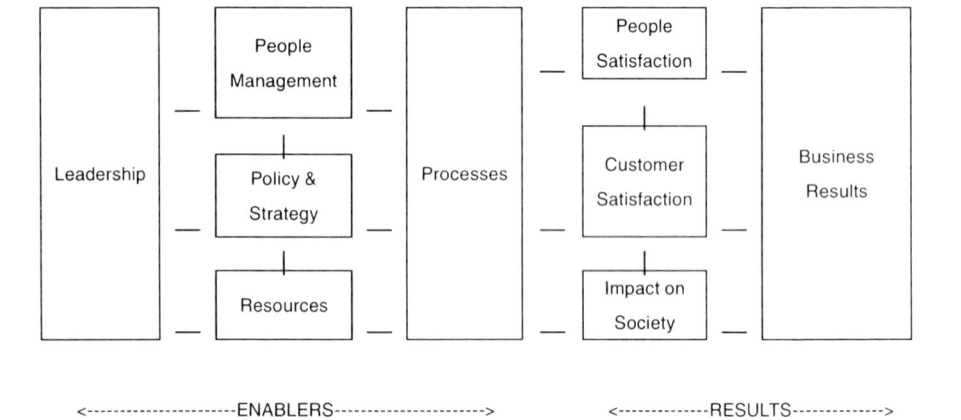

```
                    People                          People
                    Management                      Satisfaction
                         |                               |
                         |                               |
                    Policy &                        Customer
   Leadership       Strategy       Processes       Satisfaction       Business
                                                                      Results
                         |                               |
                         |                               |
                    Resources                       Impact on
                                                    Society

   <----------ENABLERS---------->       <--------RESULTS-------->
```

The BEM is made up of nine elements, divided into enablers and results. Combining this model with the car analogy above, the Business Results element is the *image* (Rolls Royce or Ford?); the Processes, along with the three elements that feed them and the three elements that stem from them, is the *product* (Silver Shadow or Cortina?). The remaining element is the *driver*—Leadership! The product and image may be great but, without a good driver, you will not get anywhere.

The BEM examines five criterion under the 'Leadership' banner, seeking to determine how the subject organisation's leaders:

- develop the mission, vision, values and ethics and are role models of a culture of excellence;
- are personally involved in ensuring the organisation's management system is developed, implemented and continuously improved;
- interact with customers, partners and representatives of society;
- reinforce a culture of excellence with the organisation's people;
- identify and champion organisational change.

I am interested to note that the fifth criterion reaffirms the view which I expressed in Chapter One, that the pace of change is now unrelenting. One phrase that is used in criterion one, above, and I do not think that I have actually used anywhere else in the book apart from the Introduction but, is one that is very relevant, is that of the leader as a role model. That very much encapsulates what I was saying in Chapter Four, about leaders understanding the significance of their actions.

DELEGATION V EMPOWERMENT

This quality culture requires that sub-ordinates have total commitment to, and ownership of, their work and delegation becomes empowerment. An interesting dichotomy for a local authority—it must embrace 'empowerment' in order to become successful in the eyes of an *autocratic* government that seeks to control it!

You may recall earlier in the book that I talked about the carrot and the stick, and went on to explain that communication and involvement are key to inspiring your team. You must work closely with your staff and listen, really listen, to what they say.

When properly involved, your staff will improve the organisation's performance dramatically. To maximise your chances of success you should delegate fully and empower slowly. The latter should be a natural evolvement of the former. Managers who have difficulty with effective delegation are likely to have serious problems with empowerment, rendering them an ineffective leader.

One definition of delegation can be 'the temporary hand-over, by a senior, to a sub-ordinate, of the command authority to carry out a task'. The 'accountability' *never* passes over; that remains with the senior. Effective delegation can be difficult to achieve but, if mastered, is a recipe for rewarding and enduring success.

Many of us have experienced, at least some of, the variety of reasons for not delegating. But is it not ironic that the main barrier to delegation—the fear of failure—inevitably increases the risk of failure and, managers who are too busy to delegate are often too busy because they do not delegate?

Some research carried out at the London Borough of Bromley in 2002 indicated that there are six styles of leadership:

- Coercive/Directive—*Do it the way I tell you.*
- Authoritative—*This is where we are going and why.*
- Affiliative—*It is important we all get on.*
- Democratic—*What do you think?*
- Pacesetting—*Watch and copy my best way.*
- Coaching—*Here is an opportunity to practise.*

What that research also showed was that pacesetting seemed to be the most dominant style used by participating managers. So, not much delegating going on, and long hours being worked. Those managers studied were 'doing' instead of leading. The other point, of course, is that none of the above six styles are wrong, unless used exclusively. What makes a really good leader is the ability to use each style appropriately.

There are numerous theories on leadership and, elsewhere, you will find authors suggesting that there are four styles, others suggesting five. So, again, nothing is right or wrong. However, I would make the point that, in addition to recognising that it is important to use each style (however many that may be) appropriately, you will need to lead groups differently to how you would lead an individual.

By virtue of being 'individual', different people will need a different mix of the aforementioned styles. As a leader, you will simply have to work that one out. As for groups, a successful approach would be achieved through taking charge of the group—bringing it together and defining objectives and roles—while empowering individuals to take responsibility on behalf of the group. I have witnessed examples of unsuccessful approaches, where the group is never brought together and individuals are brought to task when problems arise. An example of abdication by the 'leader'.

When it comes to delegation, the crux of the matter is the issue of control and 'interference'. To effectively delegate you have to create an environment whereby the sub-ordinate accepts the senior's role to advise and guide but, is left in no doubt that the senior is in charge; whilst the senior must resist the temptation to interfere unnecessarily.

Pull that little trick off and confidence on the part of both will grow, eventually nurturing the notion of 'empowerment'.

NO BLAME CULTURE

However, what is absolutely critical in this little equation is that the organisation in which you are operating has not the slightest hint of a blame culture; otherwise, the whole thing will fall at the first hurdle. There has to be an environment of mutual trust. There has to be. I make no apology for having said it again!

The leader, having identified a colleague with the appropriate aptitude for a task must trust that, once properly briefed, they will undertake it professionally and efficiently. The employee must have total confidence that their senior officer will back them fully, at least in public, and that they are there to guide and support; knowing that a monkey will not be placed on their back should anything go wrong.

After all, blaming is nothing more than a devious way of attempting to delegate accountability. Except, that is, you cannot; as we have already discussed. Blaming is simply sloping shoulders. It uses up lots of energy, but does not provide any real relief. A little bit like my rowing machine!

Do not forget that, as the leader, the buck stops with you—no-one else!

It is important to understand that point I have just made, about a leader showing public support for their team members. There is little that is more demoralising than a public admonishment. Sometimes things will not go as planned and, if a ticking-off is required, do it behind closed doors and generate a desire within the employee to learn from their mistake, not resentment.

A RECIPE FOR SUCCESS

Duncan Fletcher was replaced as England's Chief Cricket Coach in the spring of 2007. However, after a very disappointing World Cup in the Caribbean, it would be easy to forget just how instrumental Fletcher had been in guiding England from being regarded as second-rate, when he took over, to the success of being regarded as the second-best. In this situation, I do not regard second-best as failure, because England are second-best to an Australian team that is widely regarded as the best cricket team ever to have played the game. I concur totally with that assessment. So, in any other era, the current England team may well have been the best. Fletcher and the England team's success were not achieved without several years of hard-work, and an investment in a philosophy geared towards a shared vision—beating Australia!

In an article published in the Sunday Times on 26th June 2005—before England's victory in that summer's spectacular Ashes series, Fletcher outlined his ten-point recipe for success. I am not going to list them all here, just mention four but, suffice to say that, of the remaining six, five will have been specifically covered elsewhere in this book.

- First point—Never be afraid to hand responsibility to people. He says have faith in human nature. Give people a chance; they will rarely let you down.

- Second point—If you show faith in individuals, they will repay you. People generally will respond to a leader who demonstrates that they believe in them and is prepared to work with them.

Both of those points are strongly linked. They are saying be courageous, become a facilitator and an enabler. Whereas training provides the skills; leadership creates the opportunities. Give people their wings (and their 'permission to fly').

- Third point—Co-opt the rebellious by awarding them management responsibility. Fletcher believes doing so will change their character.

If you have a maverick on board, they may just be worth nurturing. This links nicely back into Chapter Two, where I was pleading not to stifle the individualism of your team; do not expect them all to adhere to the same routine and practise like robots. People with alternative views may actually force you to scrutinise something differently and, as a result, realise that you had not previously considered an important angle. It is also worth reminding yourself, at this point, that different individuals will need different guidance. Some will perform best when given complete freedom to express themselves, with no restraints; others will need very structured parameters within which to work. As a leader, you will need to work this one out, too. I would term this as pure 'man-manage-

ment', and no text book will be fully able to help prepare you for that.
- Fourth point—Listen to what the team is telling you. I have already discussed this above; listen, really listen!

I make no apology for emphasising this last point. It is important because it illustrates that real empowerment is a two-way process, where those who best know the job are truly involved.

SUCCESSION PLANNING

Finally, I would like to make one last point on this subject.

Good, effective—even transformational—leaders will be good at succession planning. And the reason is that effective delegation, which mutates into proficient empowerment, will in turn play a hugely significant role in developing the next generation of leader. Although this is a natural by-product of your successful delegation, it should always be an integral part of your strategic thinking. In simple terms, you should be preparing your natural successor, or successors if you are fortunate to be blessed with a wealth of talent; and in turn, preparing their natural successor(s).......and so on!

In what has become an ever changing, reactive world, planning is absolutely crucial to short-term attainment of targets and long-term sustained success. Do not be under any illusion that your ability as a leader will not be measured in both!

High *phat* Bites—Chapter 6

- Your product and image may be great but, without a good leader, you will not get anywhere;
- Managers who have difficulty with effective delegation are likely to have serious problems with empowerment, rendering them an ineffective leader;
- Whereas training provides the skills; leadership creates the opportunities;
- Real empowerment is a two-way process, where those who best know the job are truly involved;
- Planning is absolutely crucial to short-term attainment of targets and long-term sustained success.

Chapter 7

∽

BUSINESS PLANNING—THE MISSING LINK!

A PROPER PLAN

At the end of the previous chapter, I concluded by touching upon the strategic importance of succession planning, as a vehicle for sustained success. But, planning as a whole, not just succession planning, is critical to your effectiveness as a leader.

The planning that I am referring to, though, is not just the short-term project-based planning—which, do not get me wrong, is very important—but, the root and branch, all-encompassing, business planning. I strongly believe that not only is it virtually impossible to manage without a proper plan—whether that be a team, section, department, company or service—it is absolutely critical to have a clear Business Plan to be an effective leader.

Why? Because, it is all very well having a 'vision' but, you will not get anywhere near it without having specific aims calculated to get you there; and, even if you had those aims, they would be mere wishes if you had no explicit actions designed to achieve them.

And, in a nutshell, there you have the most basic structure and purpose of a Business Plan. Of course, in a commercial business, particularly a new one, a Business Plan is an essential requirement, otherwise you will not satisfy financial institutions, such as banks, from which you may well be seeking financial backing.

Without a Business Plan, you run the risk of:

- **F**inancial mis-management;
- drifting **A**imlessly;
- **I**ncreasing staff disillusionment, resulting in high personnel turnover; and,
- being highly reactive, much **L**ess proactive.

At this stage, can I stress that I make no apology for referring to a 'Business Plan'. I know that, in the strictest sense, a lot of the public sector is not what would be recognised as a business in the commercial sense. However, many branches of that sector are now becoming much more so, for example NHS Trusts, that it makes perfect sense for me to talk about Business Plans as being a requirement across all sectors.

BUSINESS- LIKE

In the immortal words of entertainer Max Bygraves, let me tell you a story. I go back to 1996, when I was thrust into the challenge of preparing my team for the advent of Compulsory Competitive Tendering (CCT). Termed 'Compulsory' because it had been imposed by central government. The result was that most local authorities were faced with exposing, at least, some of their white collar services to the rigours of competition, via a tendering process.

Although competitive tendering had long been established in the blue collar work that local authorities conduct, this was an alien concept to most white collar staff in the public sector. Without wishing to over-dramatise it, to begin with it was a very alarming concept. We were now being asked to compete on a commercial basis with private sector companies, and tender for the work that we were currently providing. Although the potential outcome was slightly worrying, as I delved more into it I warmed to the concept and found the learning experience extremely enlightening.

My local authority took the issue very seriously, and rightly so, and did a lot to assist in my work in ensuring we were as robust as we could be, and positioned suitably, to face the intensity of competition in a strict tendering exercise.

One way in which this was achieved was to take me away from day-to-day operational and line management responsibility, for a short while, in order to free me up to concentrate on becoming more 'business-like'. To me this was a very forward-thinking move.

Apart from providing *me* with an important opportunity, it also achieved at least two other significant advantages. In my place, a colleague had the chance to cover my post for a few months, and in turn someone covered theirs. In doing so, the responsibility was passed over but, I retained the accountability. Effective succession planning was thus expedited and empowerment, in a very tangible way, was also realised.

One task that I had to undertake as part of becoming more 'business-like' was to develop a Business Plan for the section. After a lot of background reading and research on the subject, I was having great difficulty in correlating the idea of a Business Plan to the local government environment that I was operating in.

I think I was getting bogged-down on some of the traditional aspects of a Business Plan, which did not currently have an obvious role in the work that we did—marketing is a good example of that. However, one day, I saw the light. Do you remember from your younger days, reading comics, where when a character thought of a great idea, it was depicted in the drawings by a light bulb flashing on? This was a bit like that.

I recall vividly being sat at my desk one day, when everything I had learnt from my research just fell into place. I suddenly fully understood what was required, why it was required and, most significantly, how I needed to achieve it. I guess what had happened was that I had managed to see around some of these issues which were clouding my view, and I was able to see the basic structure of a Business Plan—as mentioned earlier in this chapter—and that it was, whilst being a fairly arduous process, essentially a very simplistic concept.

I felt so liberated. I could not wait to get cracking on it! It gave me an opportunity that I had not had before. The time to analyse very carefully what we were, and were not, good at; where we needed to get to, to compete effectively; and to work out how we were going to get there. I did not do it all myself, as I will explain shortly but, the process enabled my team and I to become more creative.

A BLUE-PRINT FOR SUCCESS

Unfortunately, the current targets and inspection régime, allied to the funding mechanism that local government must adhere to, do little in my view to generate genuine innovation and creativity, merely compliance.

The answer may be to ask the public sector organisations, which do not already do so, to create proper Business Plans, as in the private sector, to illicit funding from their financiers (the Government). Each individual section and department should feed into this. All would then be given the freedom to be creative and set their own objectives, not just meeting targets set by the 'men in grey suits' in Whitehall. Maybe then the customer really would come first or, give those services the opportunity to pay some of their staff a more deserving salary. Perish the thought!

I now advocate strongly that it is difficult, if not impossible, to effectively run a sizeable organisation without having a cohesive Business Plan in place.

What I mean by cohesive is that the Business Plan should be meaningful, properly constructed and dynamic. A document to which you regularly refer, not just a mass of words put together to make it look like you have a Business Plan. Do not pay lip-service to it; it should be your blueprint to success.

Going back to my story, then, I set about working with my colleagues to construct our Business Plan. It was not going to be done by me sitting at a desk for a few hours and putting some words down on paper. I intended to do a thorough job, using a clear formula and involving the team as much as was possible.

One method that I used to achieve this was to have a staff day out of the office. Once again my employer was supportive. We booked a day in a local conference venue, closed the office, and took the whole staff complement. Taking the staff off-site is important for a number of reasons.

Firstly, because they are away from their desks it takes the staff out of their normal mind-sets, and will afford them the opportunity to be more expressive and creative. Secondly, it ensures that everyone's thought processes do not get distracted or interrupted by other issues, which occur on any given day in the workplace. Thirdly, it demonstrates that you are taking the whole process very seriously and professionally, and that you are treating your major resource (staff) accordingly. Fourthly, it is without doubt the best method of team building available—not viewed with the scepticism that can be generated by ideas such as a weekend on an assault-course.

In that conference venue, in a co-ordinated and planned way, my management team and I involved all staff in creating a main aim, setting the objectives and going a long way to putting the detailed action plans together. It was exhausting but, exhilarating. A highly rewarding experience.

I may yet write another whole book on the process, because I find it a very fascinating concept. However, I am less concerned here with *how* you do it; more, *why* you should do it!

BEGIN WITH THE END IN MIND

In a general despatch from the Institute of Human Development in 2006, they said: "Keep yourself strong through business and organisational interference and keep people focussed on the purpose of what they are doing. Purpose is the crowning responsibility of those of you who seek to be leaders in any field—purpose is the answer to the question 'why' and therefore the driving energy in organisational change and growth. Few commercial organisations can really tell us why they exist beyond profit and shareholder value and this is a meaningless vision; one that does not inspire people to go the extra mile. Companies and organisations that do have a clear sense of purpose thrive more easily than those who don't."

I think that is a wonderful, albeit slightly wordy, explanation of that enduring question: 'why?'—the answer: clear, unambiguous, purpose!

In my mind, a Business Plan is an identification of where you are now, where you want to be and, how you are going to get there. So, J.K. Rowling style, you begin with the end in mind. Where do you, or your organisation, want to go?

JK Rowling: "Begin With the End in Mind"

This can be summarised in a main aim or, mission statement, if you prefer. Whatever terminology is used and whatever it is you decide upon, it must be meaningful. Enlist the help of colleagues to toss around ideas—you could even run a competition. Although the entries are not guaranteed to come up with the actual phrase, they may well assist you in formulating what eventually becomes your main aim. A competition is also a fun way of involving staff, particularly those that may not normally be vocal but, would be prepared to write down their ideas.

The next step is to identify where you are now. One of the best ways of doing this, I would recommend, is to do a SWOT analysis (SWOT is an acronym for Strengths, Weaknesses, Opportunities, Threats). You must be prepared to be honest though. If you do this properly, it will identify very clearly and precisely what you are good at, and where you will need to improve.

Having done this, you should be able to specify your key objectives, which will enable you to meet your main aim. Or, put another way, if an objective does not help you to meet your main aim, then it probably is not a key objective. If you look carefully at your SWOT analysis, there will be themes that stand out as being the issues that need to be addressed in your objectives.

One thing that is important is that you should ensure that at least one of your objectives addresses each of the weaknesses and threats identified in the SWOT analysis, as well as taking advantage of every opportunity that was identified at that time. Having set your objectives, you now need to specify the individual, and more detailed, actions required to meet them.

HARD & SOFT SKILLS

So, it is not a simple exercise to construct a Business Plan; and it gets more complex. I have merely scratched the surface. I have not even mentioned marketing, finance, risk analysis etc. All of those issues need to be covered in a fully comprehensive Business Plan. However, as I said, my main purpose here was not to focus too much on the process but, more on what can be achieved by going through the process and producing a real plan. Business planning, properly done, involves some corporate soul-searching. It can be very tough, great fun, laborious at times but, most importantly, as I said earlier, it can be your blue-print for success.

Throughout this book, though, I have been making reference to the soft skills that you need as a leader; the people skills that will enable you to inspire, empower, nurture and drive your team to (business) fulfillment. The specialist training you have had over the years should have provided you with the necessary hard skills, the technical and management-type skills.

Business planning is almost the missing link. The welding together of all that knowledge and expertise into a single focused *plan*. Writing it is a hard skill but, you need your soft skills to generate ideas for it, to illicit appropriate input from your team members and to communicate what is in it, to make it a living breathing document. Do not underestimate its importance!

High *phat* Bites—Chapter 7

- It is absolutely critical to have a clear Business Plan to be an effective leader;
- Do not pay lip-service to it (the Plan); it should be your blue-print to success;
- Companies and organisations that do have a clear sense of purpose thrive more easily than those who do not;
- A Business Plan is an identification of where you are now, where you want to be and, how you are going to get there;
- Business planning, properly done, involves some corporate soul-searching.

Chapter 8

DO NOT COMPROMISE ON QUALITY

MEASURE OUTCOMES, NOT ACTIVITY

THE most rewarding period of my time spent in the employ of local government was when I had a Business Plan in place and my team and I were working to it. I really mean working to it, not just paying lip service to it.

Having already gone through the process that I outlined in the previous chapter; we were actually measuring progress against the action plans that we had drawn up, so that at all times we knew what we had achieved and, what we were working on. However, for me, what was most gratifying was the fact that, each time we met in our regular management meetings, we looked ahead to what we were planning to do, say, three months hence. We took time out to ensure that the foundations were in place well in advance, in order to minimise any risk that we would not deliver in the future.

It was genuinely exciting to feel that degree of control. There is always an element of reactive management but, my insistence in having a properly structured Business Plan has its roots in that experience. The benefit of controlling that which you can, as effectively as possible, means that you have a far better prospect of coping with the unexpected, when it is inevitably thrown at you, or thrust upon you.

It does not need me to remind you that most organisations do not have inexhaustible resources. The return from those limited resources needs to be maximised and, of course, the most valuable resource you have is your staff. I have, on numerous occasions, alluded to the need to cease managing and to begin leading. In Chapter Two, I briefly examined the difference between the two. What is also required is the ability to measure output and results; to measure your return on those resources, and to stop guessing; so that you have a much better idea of the full extent of that return.

Now, before I go any further, I should like to emphasise a crucially important point. What we are talking about here is performance measurement but, that does not mean that we need to work out to the exact minute the time spent by an employee at their desk; nor does it mean that we need to check rigid adherence to processes, necessarily. (Although, I do accept that in some fields, e.g. law enforcement and education, that adherence to processes is vitally, vitally important.)

You may recall that in Chapter Six I talked about nurturing any mavericks you may have in your team. What I have just said, in the paragraph above, links to that and reminds me of the following story, which is very apt.

In one particular organisation, a character spent a good deal of time looking out of the window. A new employee eventually complained to the manager, asking why this character was never brought to task and made to work like the rest. The answer was swift and certain. This character was working and once, when staring out of the window, they thought of an idea that made the organisation a small fortune!

Not something that could happen in all fields. However, the key lesson here is to understand how productive an employee is, rather than the apparent effort, necessarily. The individual in the above example may not appear to do much work in the traditional sense but, they are thinking all the time. In addition, communication is yet again critical. So that any simmering resentment may be prevented, it is essential that everyone should understand what is expected of them, as well as what is expected of everyone else, as I discussed in Chapter Three.

In the light of my experience, in terms of performance, what we should be measuring are outcomes. If you have done your business planning effectively, staff simply achieving their specified tasks will mean that the action plan is almost automatically completed; which in turn will lead to the objectives being accomplished; which in turn will achieve your main aim. The required outcomes are thus already documented.

BENCHMARKING

I have referred in Chapter Two to John Seddon's book, Freedom From Command & Control. In it he talks about the futility of both pursuing targets and measuring activity; rather than measuring outcomes.

One good way of thinking about this is to consider benchmarking, or rather the method of benchmarking. In my field, a virtual industry emerged in the 1990's with the development of benchmarking clubs, the majority of which concentrated on figures and statistical data as a comparator. This is what I viewed at the time as 'output benchmarking'. It was okay up to a point, if you were satisfied with analysing raw data. But, one problem was the continual difficulty in ensuring you were comparing 'like with like'; and even when you were sure you were, you then had to ask supplementary questions to ascertain why one set of results was so different to another.

I think 'input benchmarking'—where you are directly comparing the processes—is much more valuable and productive. Again in my own field, for instance, I am aware that Maidstone Borough Council has, in the past, done some good work in this area and has learnt a lot about customer satisfaction, from companies such as Dyson and Marks & Spencer. This makes so much more sense to me and will lend itself to achieving best practice and satisfying your main aim; the statistical results will then take care of themselves.

The result of pursuing targets, rather than measuring outcomes, is that people will focus on the activity and, cut corners. They will attempt to find ways to achieve the target, rather than accomplish the purpose. By achieving the target it may appear that a good job has been done; when in reality, the wrong thing has been done well, not the right thing being done! Cutting corners is not achieving best practice. In some industries, the consequences of cutting corners can be tragic, as I discussed earlier in the book.

Clearly, results are important. But not how you got there, nor how many coffee breaks staff had in getting you there. If you want staff to give that bit extra and go that extra mile, then you cannot treat them like children and impose strict rules and régimes on them. One way of achieving this is to involve staff in improving the processes. They do the job, so they have very valid opinions on the methodology; so, listen to them. If you are redesigning your customer reception area, ensure that staff working in that area are at the very least consulted.

FLEXIBILITY

If you want flexibility you must also be prepared to be flexible. I have always been amazed at the number of managers who shy away from ideas such as variable working hours; job-share and, most surprisingly, flexi-time. Trained and efficient staff resource can be like gold-dust. Why on Earth would you want to risk losing it through inflexibility? Just because something may be difficult in practicality, for example job-share, that is not a reason for not doing it.

In an environment that may be hugely customer-driven, it is highly likely that you will not get an even spread of work-load. So, why not use job-shares, variable hours and the other options mentioned above to your advantage, to meet that variable demand?

As for flexi-time; why, oh why, would you want to dispense with a tremendous management tool, which doubles up as a massive staff motivator? I do not need to explain that latter point but, I cannot understand why, as a manager or leader, you would want all of your team having to confront the hassle of the rush-hour each morning—arriving at work potentially stressed-out or tense, needing a few minutes to wind down. Surely it is better to give those that prefer to arrive early, to miss the rush-hour, the opportunity to do so and, to give those that prefer to arrive later, to miss the rush-hour, a similar opportunity? Giving your staff the option to arrive at work fresher and be more productive makes perfect business sense to me!

On top of that, extending the available start and end times, so that staff are not travelling to and from work during the peak rush-hour, will enable both employee and employer an opportunity to improve the environment; by reduced fumes and emissions—that can be built up during stop-start traffic—and thus, reducing their carbon footprints.

That aside, with a proper electronic clocking-on system you have all the information you need, should you be so inclined, to measure the time people are at their desk. Consequently, if you have someone that perpetually turns-in at 09:03hrs, rather than run the risk of appearing 'petty' when tackling them for being a few minutes late, the system simply records the time they are actually there for you. There are no arguments.

Beware, though. If your flexible working 'policies' are simply window-dressing with no substance or intention to adopt them, and there is no real culture of flexibility, staff can easily become cynical about such arrangements.

Efficiency has been catapulted to the very forefront of thinking. Rightly so! However, should you not be going a step or two beyond that? I cover this a little more at the beginning of Chapter Nine but, should you not be pursuing, at least effectiveness, or even excellence? Maximising the return from your resources is at the heart of all of those but, I would repeat something that I mentioned at the very start of this book. That is, whether organisations are genuinely measuring the performance of their managers.

Do they know how to? Have the required results been identified? Have they been conveyed to the post-holders? Do they know how they will be measured? All of these questions are very relevant to individual professional development. Having such a plan in place enables staff to understand the speed at which they may progress and helps to manage expectations. The manager or leader will also thus know the answer to those questions regarding themselves, once again minimising any chance of misunderstandings

As I suggested earlier, I am not talking here about whether you are performing well in comparison to your competitors, or in the government's 'league tables'. I am talking more about purpose. Your organisation's own defined purpose. Yes, I am sure you can argue hitting a target is a purpose but, what is the cost attached to that?

STRESS-CARRIERS

Does your organisation suffer from a high turnover of staff, leading to disproportionate recruitment and training costs? Are there high levels of sickness, requiring excessive expenditure on temporary staff to cover the gaps?

If the answer to those questions is 'yes', the point that I wish to make here is that good effective leaders will generally succeed in keeping sickness levels in check, simply by their words and deeds. They will create an environment where the vast majority of people want to work, and turn up, knowing that they make a difference and that it is appreciated that they make a difference.

The leader, however, must understand their potential for becoming a stress-carrier. For instance; do colleagues take one look at your frown and run for cover? Are your team afraid to walk through your door until they know you are in a reasonable mood? Unfortunately, I have met some managers who think it amusing that the answer to those two questions is 'yes'! It is no laughing matter.

Your staff spend roughly one third of their life at work; if you want them to be super-productive then *you* have to make sure that they feel as comfortable as possible. Think about the impact that your behaviour could have on them. Without compromising professionalism, try to make work fun. That does not mean that you do not take it seriously but, if people view work as an enjoyable place to be, they are much more likely to perform highly. In the first instance, they are much more likely to turn up for a start!

Going back to the subject of sickness, I have read about and understand that some organisations are now also offering 'rewards' for staff with low sickness levels. I have to say that I find this extremely difficult to accept. Why would you reward someone for simply satisfying their contract of employment and actually attending for work? If someone is 'swinging the lead' with regards to sickness, deal with that problem. I discussed the issue of dealing directly with problems, back in Chapter Four. So, whereas I can agree with, and see the arguments for, rewarding staff when they have demonstrated a desire to go that extra mile; I cannot see the virtue of rewarding staff just for getting to the start line—turning-up for work!

Having explained that I believe that it is essential to have a Business Plan (see Chapter Seven), I also believe that in order to be an effective leader you must have jurisdiction over your budget and, be able to exercise control over it. Understanding, not only the financial impact of the decisions you make but, the financial restraints that sometimes influence your decisions, ultimately makes you a more proficient and creative leader.

A comprehensive, well-structured and dynamic Business Plan will give you all the tools that you need to measure the performance of your organisation. That applies just as much in the public sector as it would in the wider business world or private sector.

In the private sector, if you get this wrong you go out of business. In the public sector, if you were in an open market, would your customers choose you, if they had a choice? You need to think in that way. The government seems relentless on measuring the minutiae, but as a leader you need to measure your real success. Quality service, delivered by quality staff, is the *only* yardstick!

High *phat* Bites—Chapter 8

- The benefit of controlling that which you can, as effectively as possible, means that you have a far better prospect of coping with the unexpected;
- It is essential that everyone should understand what is expected of them, as well as what is expected of everyone else;
- The result of pursuing targets, rather than measuring outcomes, is that people will focus on the activity and, cut corners;
- Without compromising professionalism, try to make work fun;
- In order to be an effective leader you must have jurisdiction over your budget and, be able to exercise control over it.

Chapter 9

ORGANISE YOURSELF TO SUCCESS

EFFICIENCY → EFFECTIVENESS → EXCELLENCE

SOMEONE (who operates in a management capacity) enters a room and the swing door closes behind them, just as another person is about to enter:

- A good manager (a leader) will turn and apologise immediately;
- A bad manager will simply carry on walking;
- A devious manager will turn and look to see who the person is—those they judge to be 'important' people will receive an apology; those adjudged as 'ordinary' people will just be ignored.

We have all met them, have we not? The devious type referred to above by David Jones CBE, Chairman of Next plc; the type that will look over your shoulder as you talk to them at a drinks reception, trying to spot someone that they deem to be more 'important' than you.

A real leader *believes* that everyone is important and succeeds in ensuring that everyone *knows* they are important. As I quite clearly said at the end of Chapter Eight, the *only* yardstick of real success is quality service, delivered by quality staff, and that begins right at the top!

More than once in this book I have touched upon the principle of 'doing the right thing'. Doing things right is efficiency; doing the right things is effectiveness; consistently doing the right things right is excellence; and it is that that we must all strive for. Total quality is achieved by, adding to that, the ability to produce continuous improvement through change. Not much to ask, then?

AS LUCK WOULD HAVE IT

It is not as difficult as it may sound, though. At the risk of being repetitive, the last couple of chapters in this book have majored on the critical importance of planning. Do it! When that is effectively combined with the people skills that I have largely focussed on throughout this book, the formulae is established. That is, except for one last thing: the *actual* abilities and skill-set of the workforce, including its leader.

Many, many managers—sometimes unavoidably—rely heavily on a large element of luck when it comes to their workforce. Very few are ever in the fortunate position of being involved in the recruitment, appointment and training of their entire staff. I will return to this point later in this chapter.

However, if you have had the misfortune to inherit a set of square-pegs in round holes or, more unluckily, a set of pegs for which the holes that they fit have yet to be invented, no amount of training, investment, encouragement or 'dangling of carrots' is going to produce the desired results. As the saying goes, "You can take a horse to water etc.......".

TIME MANAGEMENT

What you can do though, is learn to organise yourself in a way that will give you the best chance of generating those desired results. In other words, make sure that *you* are 'quality'!

I am not a great fan of most time management techniques. Those that know me will cry loudly, "No surprise there then!" Seriously, though, in my experience some of those techniques are actually counter-productive in the final analysis. What I mean by that is that they centre on the individual, not the team. The manager adopting them may become more effective but, not always to the benefit of their team.

For example, the growing trend of working from home. Now, occasionally, very occasionally, there may be work of critical importance that requires some quiet time to achieve, and that is fine. Provided it is occasional. Generally, a leader needs to be available; and yes, the telephone and e-mail means that they are probably always contactable but, sometimes that may not always be enough. They may need to be on the spot and, that may mean quickly! I know that what I am about to say may sound ridiculous but, often, they do not need to actually do much—just be available!

The extent of that availability will be dependent on a number of factors. These factors include the nature of the industry, the age of the organisation, its current performance level, its profitability etc. In some organisations where difficulties may exist, a new leader, for example, may need to 'dispense' their availability by actually being visible. This visibility may be necessary to build confidence and provide reassurance. So, in such circumstances, a leader working from home regularly will just not work out.

In Chapter Eight, I discussed the virtues of being flexible with working arrangements, especially in order not to miss opportunities for utilising good, well-trained, staff resource. So, your team members working from home may be a great idea. A word of warning, though. The essential rapport that needs to be built between a leader and their team cannot be done 'virtually'. It has to be real; it has to be done through direct human contact.

I am talking about eye-to-eye, face-to-face. Via text or e-mail is not sufficient. Consequently, having staff working at home will make that difficult to achieve. It is not an insurmountable problem though, as many good managers and leaders have found that they can, very successfully, lead a team spread over different locations. It can be done but, requires great determination and effective communication, from all parties, is absolutely paramount.

Another example of a time-management technique that can work against you is putting 'Do not disturb' on the door. What kind of a message do you think that this sends out to your team?

I will tell you what it says to them, 'I am far too important to be disturbed by the likes of you!"

Now, that is probably very far from the truth but, I was always told that perception is real to the perceiver so, think carefully before adopting this particular idea.

I do acknowledge that there are *some* occasions when it would be totally acceptable to use this technique. An example would be when you are conducting interviews or appraisals. However, that word 'communication' comes to mind again. In such circumstances, I would suggest that, rather than putting simply 'Do not disturb' on your door, qualify it by adding a reason why and, perhaps, a suggested time limit. That way, any visitors know that the notice is there for a good reason and, they also have a clue when may be a good time to return; which is more time efficient for all concerned.

An even more debateable example of a time-management technique that can work against you, though, is the following list of responses that could be applied if staff come to see you without an appointment:

- Ask why they are interrupting you;
- Pretend to be very busy;
- Stand during the interruption;
- Show obvious disinterest in their conversation;
- Agree with everything that is said;
- Suggest that you tackle the issue later in their office;
- Look at your watch regularly;
- Say things like "Well that solves that, then".

Those bring to my mind a certain Mr. Basil Fawlty. All designed to free you up from getting distracted but, will succeed in disengaging your member of staff. Not recommended!

There are, however, certain time management techniques that will enable managers *and* their teams to benefit. Such as, holding and attending meetings only if necessary; keeping meetings on track; preparing properly for meetings; communicating verbally in as many circumstances as possible, to allow proper feedback.

My own particular favourite has always been the use of the 'four boxes';

- Box 1—Urgent & Important
- Box 2—Urgent & Unimportant
- Box 3—Non-urgent & Important
- Box 4—Non-urgent & Unimportant.

Every task that you have fits into one of those boxes. The key to effectiveness is the content of box three. Spend the majority of your time in box three and, not only will less end up in boxes one and two but, you will organise yourself to success. You may even find that you have at least a little time for the frivolities of box four!

RECRUITMENT

At the beginning of this chapter, I mentioned that it is highly unlikely that you will ever have the chance to recruit your entire team. Given that scenario, it is absolutely vital that when recruitment opportunities come along you grab them with both hands. Make sure that you see it as exactly that....an opportunity, and do not view it as a necessary evil.

Embrace the opportunity to directly influence the make-up and personnel of your team. The odds can be stacked against you making the right choice. So, do spend time to get it right, as best you can. It is notoriously difficult to later correct errors made at the recruitment stage.

For example, research conducted in the early part of this century suggests that as many as twenty percent of candidates make some kind of false claim on their CV, or application. It is, therefore, vital to check the facts out with awarding bodies, previous employers and references. Make sure that candidates are asked to present proof of their qualifications and expertise. I have had experiences when individuals have claimed they have lost their certificates; well, ask yourself this—if they are so careless with their own important possessions, how reliable are they going to be in the event that you charge them with your organisation's interests?

For some time now, the insurance industry has made use of Voice Recognition Analysis (VRA) systems to ascertain whether telephone claimants are genuine. This tool has proven to be highly accurate and very successful for them. As I write, VRA is being trialled in the field of benefit claims, in an attempt to reduce the proportion of fraudulent claims. My thought was, why not use it as part of the recruitment process? A step in that procedure could be introduced where all potential candidates were called up on the telephone and asked to talk about their qualifications and experience; it might give you a strong clue as to whether anyone is potentially bending the truth, shall we say?

If you are appointing to a position which has line management responsibility, it is essential that your recruitment process is as rigorous as it can be. I would recommend that merely an application and an interview is woefully inadequate when assessing an individual's leadership potential. Psychometric tests can be a useful additional tool and give an insight into personality; assessment centres and your own individually designed tests can assist in measuring technical expertise; and, I would certainly not advise against utilising any opportunity for candidates to meet with potential colleagues, providing that the meeting is appropriately structured.

One other option that has become available—and the jury is currently out as to its credence—is to do a search of candidates on the internet. On the one hand, this is potentially 'dangerous', in that you may find out some irrelevancies about individuals which cloud your judgement; on the other hand, the more you can learn about an individual before appointing them will minimise the risk of costly errors. I would seek specialist HR advice on this particular option before committing to using it.

All too often, you may feel pressurised to make a quick appointment, maybe to appease pressure from your staff, colleagues or senior officers. Do not be tempted to cut corners. A few days spent checking the facts before making a job offer, can avoid weeks of grief and pain trying to get someone to 'toe the line' later.

I once recall being asked for a day off by a temporary worker back in the days of Community Charge (or Poll Tax); only to discover that the reason they wanted a day off was to attend court for their involvement in the Trafalgar Square Poll Tax riots. Can you imagine what fun the local press and some politicians would have had, as well as the scorn from the public; had such a story become public? Suffice it to say that the individual concerned was advised not to return, and our vetting procedures were somewhat tightened!

RETENTION

It does not end there either. This principle of ensuring that staff understand their importance to the organisation was discussed in depth in Chapter Five of this book. I did not, at that point, extend the argument, as it were.

In 2002, the Audit Commission published a survey, 'Recruitment and Retention: a public workforce for the 21st Century'. In it they describe how employers do not know why their staff are leaving. They found that less than one in five of people surveyed had had an exit interview when they left their public sector job. I find that quite staggering.

How on Earth are you expected to know what is and is not working, when you do not ask the people most likely to tell you, honestly? I discovered at one authority I worked at that HR were selective of who they interviewed so, upon discovering that fact, I made a point of ensuring that I interviewed *every* person who left my team. I was also staggered to find that another organisation did not, as a matter of course, give general feedback to team managers on their findings from exit interviews.

So, given that, what was the real benefit of doing them? Clearly, they have to protect the confidentiality of the interviewee but, there is nothing wrong with general feedback to the appropriate person. So, even if something detrimental, or of concern, had come to light about the individual to whom the feedback were normally given, it can be given to their senior officer as an alternative. This obviously raises the important point; accept that in an exit interview you may hear something that you did not want to. But, if you want to get things right and succeed, you have to be prepared for that.

If your HR department does not conduct exit interviews for every single employee who leaves, then might I suggest that you find time to do it yourself? You may be amazed at what you find out. And, guess what? This task fits into box three!

High phat Bites—Chapter 9

- Doing things right is efficiency; doing the right things is effectiveness; consistently doing the right things right is excellence;
- Generally, a leader needs to be available;
- Spend the majority of your time in box three and, not only will less end up in boxes one and two but, you will organise yourself to success;
- Embrace the opportunity to directly influence the make-up and personnel of your team;
- Accept that in an exit interview you may hear something that you did not want to.

Chapter 10

BE TRUE TO YOURSELF

AUTHENTICITY

"Always be true to yourself, my son, for there is greatness within you." Many of you will be familiar with that famous enunciation, attributed to film producer Bill Cross. The full version actually ends with the line, "Don't be satisfied with less than all you can be, for you have greatness within you."

Throughout the previous chapters, in this book on the subject of leadership, I have covered a range of topics aimed at identifying what makes a transformational or inspirational leader, and how that is so different to 'management'.

It is not easy to be a leader, and what Bill Cross is saying is do not settle for second best, do not settle for anything less than what you should be but, most importantly, do not compromise yourself or your beliefs. The attributes of leadership can be honed and developed but, you must be true to yourself because, if you do not believe in what you are doing, it will be as transparent as a politician's promise!

Although the author G.K. Chesterton once said that 'The men who really believe in themselves are all in lunatic asylums'; I do not allow that to influence my conviction that it is possible to aspire to greatness.

In his book, Authentic Leadership, Bill George strongly reaffirms this concept of being true to yourself. He advocates that you must understand your purpose; practise solid values; establish connected relationships; demonstrate self-discipline and lead with your heart. I could not agree more, particularly with that last point. Your heart will instinctively tell you what is right and what is wrong in most circumstances. Trust it.

In Chapter Six, I mentioned a variety of leadership styles and discussed that, used in moderation, all are acceptable. It is important that you understand which your dominant style is and, that you learn when it is appropriate to use the other styles.

To do that, good judgement is required; this comes from experience. Unfortunately, it cannot really be helped but, experience comes from, amongst other things, bad judgement! That is why it is important that, as a leader you allow your staff the space to make their mistakes, from which they can learn; in the same way that you must learn from your own. What you cannot do, and must not try to do, is turn yourself into someone else. What I mean by that is that you cannot change your personality.

What you should try and learn to do is use some of those characteristics which are less like you and apply them appropriately for short periods. The following tale is an example of where I applied that strategy.

I have referred before to the time when I was leading a team into a tendering exercise. As time passed, the enormity of the task ahead was becoming all too apparent. On one occasion, I became worried by the prospect of making a presentation, about my team's tender, to the Elected Members of our local authority. I had no experience of anything on that scale, particularly knowing that our future employment may depend upon how successful my presentation was. I considered what options were available to me to enable me to gain experience of that nature.

The only answer I could come up with was to volunteer to make a presentation at the annual conference of my professional body, The Institute of Revenues, Rating & Valuation (IRRV). So, that is exactly what I did; I put myself right under the microscope by presenting a paper on my experiences of preparing for that tendering exercise, to an estimated audience of three hundred people at conference in Eastbourne. It was an incredibly daunting experience but, one from which I learnt a great deal about myself.

So, you are what you are, and you cannot force yourself to be, perhaps, someone more dynamic or charismatic. Authenticity is of paramount importance; any lack of it will be all too evident. What you can do, is not be afraid to learn to be adaptable.

In the previous chapters, I have covered everything from generating inspiration, as opposed to motivation; the importance of professionalism and integrity; the impact of your words and deeds; how essential team work is; the significance of effective empowerment; the value of proper planning; through to the necessity for quality at all levels.

In doing so, I have deliberately avoided detailed reference to some of the established management thinkers and their techniques. There is immense merit in considering the theories expounded by the likes of Machiavelli and modern day practitioners such as Tom Peters. However, as I said, this series has been more about leadership and, rather than theoretical techniques, I would like to think it has been a consideration of a common-sense approach. An approach where instinct and humanity—with not a little humility—are at the forefront. Use your head……..and lead with your heart!

THE FOUR FRAMEWORKS FOR SUCCESS

Having said that, I should like to bring this book to a conclusion by mentioning four frameworks which I believe can be valuable as a reference for aspiring leaders. It can sometimes be comforting or reassuring to have a 'toolbox', to which you can return from time to time.

These 'frameworks' first came to my attention in an article by Michael Useem, Professor of Management at The Wharton School, University of Pennsylvania, published in the Financial Times in November 2000.

Framework One is called 'the three-part story'. Leaders such as Margaret Thatcher and Nelson Mandela were adept at the use of this. Great leaders effectively convey their vision of what should be and how it should be achieved but, there is a key third part, which is harnessing the people that they lead, to build that future.

Mandela, for instance, declared long before it happened, that the people of South Africa would create a multi-racial, democratic nation. I guess this links back into what I was saying in Chapter Three, about great leaders being able to draw upon people's emotions to inspire them. Mandela was highly skilled in this art.

Margaret Thatcher: "The Three-part Story"

Framework Two is called 'the teachable point of view'. This has been defined as 'what you want your organisation to achieve and how it will do so'. What is important here is that the message must be conveyed in a form that others can readily learn and, in turn, pass on. Use 'real' language and your message will be transmitted more clearly and, possibly, viewed with less scepticism. Avoid the perils of using 'management speak' and jargon when communicating with your staff. Doing so may be translated, by them, as masking a hidden agenda.

It is vital that the right leaders are chosen, so that they master their responsibilities, both operationally and developmentally. The saying goes that it is not the business that grows but, the people in it! However, that will only happen if the leaders have the aptitude to nurture and develop their team members.

Framework Three is termed 'the other intellect'. Most responsible positions require a certain level of knowledge and/or experience. But, what distinguishes the true leader is a level of 'emotional intelligence'. I discussed the meaning of this in more detail in Chapter Five, and I mentioned there that Daniel Goleman explained that self-awareness, self-regulation, empathy and compassion; combined with an ability to bring out the best in people, means that a leader will hear what they need to know and inspire others in what they need to do.

Some people are fortunate enough to have innate 'emotional intelligence', others not so. However, it can be developed through experience........which, as I said earlier, comes from bad judgement. So, be prepared to make a few errors along the way but, learn from them.

All of the things that the above frameworks refer to, have been touched upon at some point earlier in this book. But, it is Framework Four that is the one that I most identify with and want to look more closely at.

It is called 'the seventy percent solution'. Some institutions are renowned for their excellence in leadership. Useem said that one such is the US Marine Corps; although I guess that some people in the world would now question that organisation's strategies at times! However, when it comes to leadership, the US Marine Corps use the following principles:

- seek a 70% solution, rather than a 100% consensus;
- avoid indecisiveness, no decision is worse than a weak decision;
- clearly explain the objectives of a decision, then allow subordinates to work out the details;
- tolerate and even encourage mistakes, where they can generate better performance next time;
- prepare everybody to lead.

In summary, what this means is that with any group of human beings, you will never get a one hundred percent consensus, so seventy percent is a good result. Go with it. It is a little bit like 'Ask the audience' in the TV programme "Who Wants to be a Millionaire?" It is worth bearing in mind that, generally, democratic leaders will not necessarily be seeking consent but, will be looking for commitment to their vision. A subtle difference.

Indecisiveness can be fatal in the armed forces but, in the 'business-world' it can still be crippling. This links directly back to Chapter One, where I talked about the Second Derivative—your ability to accelerate to capture opportunity. Do not prevaricate, think smartly—act quickly, not hastily. Do not be under the misapprehension that all the detail must be known before a decision can be taken. Communicate the thinking with the decision; if your staff know why it is so, they are more likely to respond favourably and they can work out the detail.

Give your team the opportunity to learn and to develop, and do not look to apportion blame every time there is a mistake. Use it as a learning experience and an opportunity.

Finally, what the fourth framework teaches is, prepare everyone to lead. There may be occasions when certain circumstances require a different skill set to your own. It is not a weakness to allow one of your team to take the lead on those occasions. Recognising those occasions is a strength of good leadership, not a sign of weak leadership.

If you are, or become, an effective leader, I believe that if you analyse your approach to a variety of situations and circumstances, one of the above four frameworks will always be strongly evident.

THE 'COOL' LEADER (PHAT CONTROLLER)

Many see 'leadership' as power. To a certain extent it is but, the real power is in influencing people, not controlling them. Many use knowledge as power, seeking to keep others in the dark. This, though, is controlling; and, I am afraid to say, belies a deep insecurity in the individual who is seeking to 'control'. Real power is using your knowledge to influence and to inspire. Share your knowledge, share your power—communicate fully and effectively, and you will be astonished and impressed with the results.

Several years ago I was, quite literally, blown over by the wind whilst attending to my work in Basingstoke. At the time, I was carrying a long box, which acted as a sort of wind-sock; walking along the road, a strong gust of wind suddenly swept me off my feet and deposited me, unceremoniously, on the floor. I was stunned and, slightly injured. Ever since that incident, I have held an irrational, but very real, fear of the wind. In 2006, whilst on holiday on the Greek island of Kos, in very hot temperatures I remember being cooled by the breeze. It was very soothing.

Being in such a relaxed environment, it allowed me the space to stop and think about how the effects of, what is essentially, the same phenomenon can be so different as to create results that are literally poles apart.

Management and leadership can be like that, I concluded.

As the esteemed American political writer, Walter Lippmann, once said: "The final test of a leader is that he leaves behind him in other men the conviction and the will to carry on!"

There is no need to be afraid of failure but, do have sufficient fear that you have the humility to succeed. Do not be a manager who blows like the wind and whose power is fear. Be a leader, cool as the breeze, whose power is calming and reassuring!

High *phat* Bites—Chapter 10

- The attributes of leadership can be honed and developed but, you must be true to yourself;
- Use your head……and lead with your heart;
- Avoid the perils of using 'management speak' and jargon when communicating with your staff;
- Give your team the opportunity to learn and to develop, and do not look to apportion blame every time there is a mistake;
- Real power is using your knowledge to influence and to inspire.

Acknowledgements & References:

In writing this book, I have used a number of reference points and a variety of publications as source documents. I should like to take the opportunity to hereby acknowledge the contributions made by those organisations responsible.

Authentic Leadership; *Bill George* (Jossey-Bass)
Business Excellence Model (European Foundation for Quality Management)
Coronation Street (ITV Productions)
Dead Poets Society (Touchstone Pictures)
Denis Beard, Director of Management, University of Reading
Emotional Intelligence; *Daniel Goleman* (Reed Business Information Inc.)
Freedom From Command & Control….a Better Way to Make the Work Work; *John Seddon* (Vanguard Press)
Harry Potter and The Chamber of Secrets (Warner Brothers)
Harvard Business Review (Harvard Business School Publishing)
How to Win Friends and Influence People; *Dale Carnegie* (Simon & Schuster)
Imagine; *John Lennon* (Parlaphone)
John Laing & Son Ltd. v. Kingswood Area A.C. (1949)
Leadership; *R.Wheatley & C.Smith* (The Institute of Management Foundation)
Leadership….with a Human Touch (Economics Press UK Ltd.)
Local Government Chronicle (eMap Public Sector Publications)
MacFarlane (Leadership) Ltd.
Photographic illustrations courtesy of Getty Images
Rating Law & Practice; *Textbook* (Institute of Revenues, Rating & Valuation)
Recruitment and Retention: A Public Workforce for the 21st Century (Audit Commission)
The Celestine Prophecy; *James Redfield* (Warner Books Inc.)
The Financial Times (Financial Times Ltd.)

The Institute of Human Development
The Lord of the Flies; *William Golding* (Faber & Faber)
The Oxford English Dictionary (Oxford University Press)
The Seven Habits of Highly Effective People; *Stephen Covey* (Simon & Schuster)
The Sunday Times (News International Group)
Timeless Values (Helen Exley Giftbooks)
www.wikipedia.org (on-line Encyclopedia)

Index

Akabusi, Kris	18
Altruism	31
Appleyard, Keith	41
Appraisals	19; 43; 81
Armstrong, Neil	23
Ashes, *The*	60
Audit Commission, *The*	84
Australia	60
Authentic Leadership	87
Balanced Scorecard (BSC)	56
Basingstoke, Hants, UK	92
Beard, Denis	34
Benchmarking	72
Benefits Agency, *The*	29
Best Value	55
Black, Roger	16-18
Body Language	35
Brighton, West Sussex, UK	16
Bromley, London Borough of, UK	58
Bullying	20; 28
Business Excellence Model (BEM)	56
Business Plan	19; 63-70; 71-72; 76
Business (Non-Domestic) Rates	16; 52
Bygraves, Max	64
Caribbean, The	59
Carnegie, Dale	41-42
Carrot or Stick	28; 31-32; 49; 57
Celestine Prophecy, The	47
Chamber of Secrets, The	40
Character Ethic	42; 45
Chesterton, GK	87

Christian faith	11
Christmas	35; 51
Churchill, *Sir* Winston	34
Clough, Brian	31
Command & Control	25-26; 28; 30; 33; 50
Communication	34-36; 37; 57; 72; 81-82; 92
Community Charge (Poll Tax)	15; 41; 84
Comprehensive Performance Assessment (CPA)	55
Compulsory Competitive Tendering (CCT)	55; 64
Coronation Street	41
Council Tax	15-16; 49; 52
Covey, Stephen	42-43
Cricket World Cup	59
Cross, Bill	87
Cumbrian Rail Disaster	26
Dead Poets Society	28
Definition (of leadership)	23
Delegation	57-59; 61-62
Derby County AFC	31
Dumbledore, *Professor*	40
Dyson	73
Eastbourne, East Sussex, UK	88
Economics Press (UK) Ltd.	39
Emotional Intelligence	47-48; 91
Emotions	32-34; 36; 93
Empowerment	57-59; 61-62; 65; 88
Esprit de Corps	12-13
European Foundation for Quality Management (EFQM)	56
Exit Interviews	84-86
Failure demand vs. Value demand	29-30
Fawlty, Basil	82
Ferguson, *Sir* Alex	31

Financial Times, *The*	18; 89
Fletcher, Duncan	59-60
Ford Cortina	55-56
Four Boxes, *The*	82
Four Frameworks, *The*	89-92
Fraud	49
Freedom from Command & Control....	25; 72
Fuhrüngskunst	23
General Practitioner (GP)	16
General Rates	16
George, Bill	87
Gershon, *Sir* Peter	55
Ghandi, Mahatma	44
Giuliani, *Mayor* Rudolph	10
Golden Rule, *The*	41-42
Golding, William	50
Goleman, Daniel	47-48; 91
Gosport, Hampshire, UK	16
Harvard Business *Review, The*	32
Health & Safety	20; 26
Herzberg, Frederick	32
Hierarchical Structures	26; 41; 48; 50; 55
Housing Benefits	29; 49; 52; 83
Hovis	16
How to Win Friends and Influence People	41
Imagine	46
Input benchmarking	73
Inspiration	32; 36-37; 54; 87-88
Institute of Human Development, *The*	19; 67
Institute of Revenues, Rating & Valuation, *The*	9; 88
Integrity	24-25; 30; 36; 42-43; 88
International Organisation for Standardisation (ISO)	55
Investors in People	19
ITV	41

John Laing & Son Ltd.	16
Jones, David	79
Keane, Roy	31
Keating, *Prof.* John	29
King Jr., Martin Luther	33-34
Kos, Greece	92
Laird, Dr Donald A.	24; 26
Lennon, John	47; 51-52
Lippmann, Walter	93
Lord of the Flies; The	50
Low-Hanging Fruit	42-43
Machiavelli	89
Maidstone Borough Council, Kent, UK	73
Management	15; 20; 23-24; 42; 55-56; 87; 88-89; 93
Managing Upwards	26-27
Manchester United AFC	31
Mandela, Nelson	89
Marks & Spencer	73
Morale	35; 37
Motivation	13; 32; 37; 88
Muslim faith	11
Muzyka, Dr Daniel	18
Next PLC	79
NHS Trusts	64
New York, USA	11
Non Domestic (Business) Rates	16; 52
Nottingham Forest AFC	31
Oxford English Dictionary, *The*	23
Other Intellect, *The*	91
Output benchmarking	73
Performance Indicators	17; 28
Performance Management	14; 19; 72; 76

Personality Ethic	42
Peters, Tom	89
Poll Tax (Community Charge)	15; 41; 84
Potter, Harry	40
Professional Development Plans	32; 37; 75
Professionalism	43-44; 76; 77; 88
Rating Law & Practice	16
Reagan, Ronald	13
Recruitment	82-84
Redfield, James	47
Redmond, Derek	18
Regis, John	18
Role Models	12-13; 57
Rolls Royce Silver Shadow	55-56
Rowling, JK	67-68
Royal Navy, The	50
Sadat, Anwar	42
Scargill, Arthur	34
Second Derivative	18-19; 92
Seddon, John	25; 28-29; 72
Seven Habits of Highly Effective People, The	42
Seventy Percent Solution, The	91-92
Society of Chief Personnel Officers, The	16
South Africa	89
Stealth	25
Stress-carrier	41; 75-76
Styles of leadership	58; 87-88
Succession Planning	61; 63; 65
Sunday Times, The	60
Sunderland AFC	31
SWOT Analysis	68-69
Synergy	50
Teachable Point of View, The	90
Team Work	48; 50; 54; 88
Television (TV)	13; 16; 41; 91
Terrorism	11-12

Thatcher, Margaret	13; 16; 89-90
Three-part Story, *The*	89
Time management	80-82
Tokyo, Japan	16-18
Total Quality Management (TQM)	55
Trade Union	34
Trafalgar Square, London, UK	84
Transient Occupation	16
US Marine Corps	91
University of British Columbia, Canada	18
University of Pennsylvania, USA	89
University of Reading, Berks, UK	34
Useem, Michael	89; 91
Value for Money	55
Vancouver, Canada	18
Varney, Sir David	56
Voice Recognition Analysis (VRA)	83
Walk the Talk	41; 49
Weber, Max	48
Whitehall, London, UK	66
Who Wants to be a Millionaire?	91
Wikipedia	47
World Athletics Championships	16-18
Williams, Robin	29
World Trade Center, New York, USA	11

ENDS